I am the Door

Exploring the Christ Presence

Within

Book Design
by Paul Ferrini and Lisa Carta
Thanks to Don Stewart for Copy Editing

Front cover painting: *Christ at Thirty-three,*
by Heinrich Hofman, used by permission of Riverside Church
and New York Graphic Society
Back cover photo of entrance to Santuario de Chimayo,
Chimayo, New Mexico, by Mark Caryl.

Library of Congress Catalog Card Number: 99-90530
ISBN 1-879159-41-4

Manufactured in the United States of America

HEART WAYS
PRESS

P.O. Box 99
Greenfield, MA 01302

I am the Door

Exploring the Christ Presence Within

Paul Ferrini

Table of Contents

The Gift

The Gift

God gave you one gift for your journey and one gift alone. He said: "My Son, remember, you can change your mind at any time."

He did not say: "Do not leave, Son." He did not say "Son, you will be miserable until you return to Me." He just said: "Remember, you can change your mind at any time."

You can change your mind about every painful and unforgiving thought that you think. You can question each unhappy thought and think another thought that releases you and brings joy into your heart.

God did not say: "I will not let My Son make mistakes." He said: "I trust in your return and I give you a gift to see you home."

All your mistakes mean nothing to God. To Him, you are but a child exploring your world and, through trial and error, learning the rules that govern it.

God did not make those rules. You made them. You forgot only one thing, and God gave that to you with his blessing. He said: "No matter where your journey takes you, Son, remember, you can change your mind at any time."

With a single loving thought, He made temporal what

you would make final. He made unreal what you would make real.

You created the ashes of death. He created the wings of the phoenix. To every unhappy thought you would think, God gave a single answer. "Remember, Son, you can change your mind at any time."

Like Prometheus, you tried to steal the fire of the gods. But He did not punish you for this. He did not chain you to the rock where you would live throughout all eternity with vultures as your only playmates. He said: "take the sacred fire, Son, but be careful, and remember you can change your mind at any time."

Like Adam and Eve, you stood in the garden and became curious about good and evil. When He knew your desire for knowledge would not pass, He sent the sacred snake to you with an apple and invited you to eat. Contrary to popular opinion, He did not trick you into sin and then banish you from the garden. He just said: "Be careful, my Son. When you eat this fruit, your perception of the world will change. This garden may suddenly seem a dry desert where nothing grows at all. Your body with all its innocent grace may seem to be a home for dark desires of which you are ashamed. Your mind, which now shares my every thought, may seem to think thoughts opposed to mine. Duality and feelings of separation may seem to enter your consciousness and experience. All this and more may arise from this tiny bite you would eat, but remember, Son, you can change your mind at any time."

Not only does God not condemn you for your mistakes, He is not concerned about them. He knows the child will burn itself with an open flame. But He also knows the child will learn to keep the flame carefully and use it to warm himself and light his way.

He knows that your decision "to know" will bring you into dangerous situations, situations when you think your happiness depends on the way another treats you, situations in which you forget you are not a vulnerable organism in an arid and hostile land.

He knows that you will forget your origin, and that there will be times in which the Garden seems but a distant memory, whose very existence is questionable. He knows that there will be times in which you blame Him for all of your troubles and forget that you were the one who chose "to know." But all this does not concern Him. Because, before you left hell-bent on your journey of separation, He said: "just a minute, Son. It may be a long time before we meet again. Won't you please accept this simple gift from me, and keep it wherever you go in remembrance of me?"

Most of you do not remember answering "Yes, Father." But I assure you that you did. And so the voice of God went with you as you went into exile. And it is still with you now.

So, when you feel forlorn and lost, when you forget that you chose this journey, remember "You can change your mind at any time." I am here to help you remember that.

This is not my gift, but God's gift to you. Because I received the gift from Him, I can give it to you. And if you receive it of me, you can give it to your brother or sister.

But I caution you, do not be concerned with the identity of the giver. I am not important. I am not the gift, but the one who extends it, as indeed are you. Let us remember the origin of the gift so that we can give it and receive it freely.

God gave you the gift of forgiveness. This gift travels with you wherever you go. When you do not trust it, he sends His Son to you to remind you of the gift.

Many beings of light have come as the Christ, bringing that simple reminder. All have the same purpose, for

Christ is not a person, but a keeper of the flame, a giver of the gift, and a messenger of love. Light comes from him, because he has remembered light in the darkness of the world. Love comes from him, because he has received the gift and learned to give it unconditionally to all who would receive it.

You are the Door

You are the Door

You have heard me say, "I am the way, the truth and the life." That statement is equally true for you. The truth, the path to the divine, the life of the witness runs through your heart. There is no way, no truth, no life, except through you.

You have focused so much on how great I am, you have forgotten your own greatness. You have neglected the fact that forgiveness cannot be offered to the world except through you.

Take me down from the pedestal, my brother or sister, and place me at your side, where I belong. I am your absolute, unconditional equal. What I have done, you too will do.

You will not be saved by my thoughts and actions, but by your own. Except you become Christ, peace will not come to the world.

You are not a victim of the world, but the one who holds the key to freedom. In your eyes is the spark of divine light that leads all beings out of the darkness of fear and mistrust. And in your heart is the love that gives birth to all the myriad beings in the universe.

Your essence is unbroken, whole, dynamic and creative. It but awaits your trust.

Neither Mary nor I is more spiritual than you are. We are like you in every way. Your pain is our pain. Your joy is our joy. If this were not true, we could not come to teach.

Do not hold us at arm's length. Embrace us as your equal. Mary could have been your mother. I could have been your son.

⁂

When you think of me, do not dwell on the "miraculous" things I have done. The power of love will make miracles in your life as wonderful as any attributed to me. For love is the only miracle, not you or I.

Let us not take credit for what love has done or will do. The credit belongs to the one who loved us without conditions long before we knew what love was, or what its absence would mean to us.

⁂

You are one facet in the many-faceted jewel of God's love and grace. The beauty of one facet does not interfere with the splendor of another, but adds to it in both breadth and intensity. What makes one facet shine is available to all. The light that is in me is also in you.

⁂

I offer you a living teaching, not just a set of abstract beliefs. Following me means more than preaching my words. It means following my example.

Look to my example, not to worship me, but to understand what is possible for you.

There is no one who will refuse love when it is offered without conditions. And who will offer it but you, my brother or sister?

Today you will drink deeply from the fountain of my love. Tomorrow you will be the fountain.

The Desire to Communicate with Me

Each of you has available to you a personal relationship with me. That relationship comes into being simply as you begin to want it and trust it. The simple but authentic need for my friendship is all that is required.

The desire to communicate with me is essential to opening the door to my presence.

I am as close to you as you would have me be. That is because I am already a thought within your mind. And everything that I am proceeds from that thought, just as everything I am not proceeds from a different thought.

I am a thought without limitation, for I am ever expanding into the formlessness of God. There is no form that can contain me. I have joined with God in perfect forgiveness. I am free of guilt. I am free of grievances. I do not believe that I can be wronged, nor do I believe that I have the power to wrong another.

It is in your thoughts that you choose to walk with me or to walk away from me. If you would be like me, you must learn to think like me. Unhelpful thoughts must be witnessed lovingly and gently released. Then, only thoughts that bless and recall you to truth will remain.

You are all masters at taking truth and inverting it. But just because you have inverted truth does not mean the truth ceases to be true. It means only that you have succeeded in hiding the truth from yourself.

My teaching has been and will continue to be distorted because it threatens every thought that is false. This is why I ask you to be vigilant. A single false idea can bring the mind that thinks it to despair. But a single true thought restores the kingdom.

Truth is an Open Door

Truth is a door that remains open. You cannot close this door. You can choose not to enter. You can walk in the opposite direction. But you can never say: "I tried to enter, but the door was closed." The door is never closed to you or anyone else.

It is not necessary to seek God, because God is already the essence of who you are. Simply remove all judgments and thoughts that do not bless you and others. Then the veil will be lifted and only God will remain.

As illusions are surrendered, truth appears. As separation is relinquished, the original unity emerges unchanged. When you stop pretending to be what you are not, what you are can be clearly seen.

Christ is the Friend

The Friend is the Christ within you. It doesn't matter what you call him or her. The Friend is the one who has your greatest good at heart. The Friend is the one who also has the greatest good of others at heart.

The Friend is the one who is free of judgment, the one who accepts you and everyone else unconditionally. This Friend is within every mind and heart.

The Friend is the embodiment of love. S/he has many names and faces.

God and the Friend are always one. When you approach the Friend within, God hears your footsteps.

The Original Spark of Creation

Within your heart and mind right now is the original spark of Creation. It belongs to you and can never leave you. No matter where your life takes you, no matter how far you stray from the path, you cannot extinguish the spark of divinity within your own consciousness. It was and is God's gift to you.

You can forget about the gift but you cannot give it back. You can ignore or deny it, but you cannot un-create it. The deeper the darkness through which you walk, the more visible the tiny spark becomes. It calls to you like a beacon reminding you of your essence and your place of origin.

When you acknowledge the spark and nurture it, the light within you grows. The more attention you give to it, the more it expands until your whole being is surrounded by light. Even total strangers feel the rays of your love touching them.

Then you too become the Friend, the Christ, the Buddha, the Compassionate One.

The Light of Truth

The light of truth lives even in the darkest of places. There is no such thing as total absence of light. Darkness cannot exist except in reference to the light. All darkness is a journey toward light. No matter how great your pain, it is measured by the degree to which you feel love's absence or loss. All pain is a journey toward love without conditions.

You are here to enter the darkness you see in yourself and others and find the light that lives there. Once you find the light, no matter how insignificant it seems, your life will never be the same. A light bearer never questions the light s/he carries. And so s/he can offer it to others patiently and without fear.

Words and Concepts

Words and beliefs that separate you from others must be put aside. If you wish to walk in peace, find what you share with others and overlook the differences you see.

※

God has many ways of bringing us home. Do not think that those who follow a different path home will be denied salvation.

Truth comes in all shapes and sizes, but it remains one simple truth. You must learn to see the truth in every form, in each situation.

The Language of Love

Your love expresses itself regardless of what you believe. The language of love is not a language of words.

Words and concepts will not open your heart. Only love can open your heart.

When love is in your heart, the path opens before you. Actions flow spontaneously from you. There is no self-consciousness, ambivalence, or deliberation. For these are not the qualities of love.

Spirituality

Spirituality and religion are not necessarily the same thing. Religion is the outer form; spirituality is the inner content. Religion is the husk; spirituality is the seed. Religion is a set of beliefs; spirituality is a continuum of experience.

To be spiritual is to see without judgment, to see not just with the eyes, but with the heart. When you look with the heart, you see beauty everywhere, even in suffering. Wherever hearts are touched by the poignancy of life, there is beauty. There is beauty in the rain and clouds, and beauty in the sunlight. There is beauty in aloneness and in intimacy, in laughter and in tears.

God's Children

You are God's child, even as I am. All that is good and true about God is good and true about you. Accept this fact, even for an instant, and your life would be transformed. Accept this about your brother or sister, and all conflict between you would end.

In your interactions, you have a simple choice: to find each other innocent or to find each other guilty. This choice occurs over and over again, every day, every hour, every moment. Thought by thought, you imprison each other or release each other. And as you choose to treat others, so do you deliver the same judgment upon yourself.

Every judgment you make about your brother or sister states very specifically what you cannot accept about yourself. You never judge or dislike another person unless s/he reminds you of yourself.

Mistakes

Your awareness of your mistakes is a gift because it brings you to correction.

When you justify your mistakes, you hang onto them, forcing yourself to defend your actions over and over again. This takes a great deal of time and energy. Indeed, if you are not careful, it can become the dominant theme of your life.

Admit your mistakes and deliver yourself from pain, struggle, and deceit. There is no mistake that cannot be corrected. There is no trespass that cannot be forgiven.

To be mistaken is not such a terrible a thing. It will not deprive you of love and acceptance. What deprives you of love is your insistence on being right when you are not. That prevents correction from being made.

Be humble, my friend. Unless you recognize that you have made a mistake, how can you correct it? But admit your mistake and correction will be there, along with forgiveness. That is the path I have set out for you.

Give Forgiveness, Not Guilt

Mistakes are opportunities for learning. To condemn your sister for making mistakes is to pretend to be mistake-free, which you are not. I have asked you before and I will ask you again: which one of you will throw the first stone?

Instead of condemning your sister for her mistakes, release her from your judgment. To release her is to love her, for it places her where love alone lies, beyond judgment of any kind.

＊

To make wrong is to teach guilt and perpetuate the belief that punishment is necessary. To make right is to teach love and demonstrate forgiveness. To put it simply, you are never right to make wrong, or wrong to make right. To be right, make right.

You cannot love in an unloving way. You can't be right and attack what's wrong.

＊

When you become burdened by the affairs of the world, take sanctuary in a quiet place. Let go of your worries and fears about the future. Stop clinging to your guilt about what you have said and done in the past.

Let your heart be mended. Then you can make amends with anyone you have treated unkindly.

Learn to forgive yourself. No matter what you have said or done, you do not deserve to suffer. Your suffering will not feed the hungry or heal the sick.

Forgive and come back into your life with a clear vision and a strong heart. Your freedom from guilt serves not just you, but also those who need your kind deeds and your compassionate understanding.

Evil is An Illusion

People aren't born with error. Take any baby and love it and nurture it and give it wings and it will be a beacon of love. But take the same baby and withhold love from it and refuse to encourage it, and you will be sowing the seeds of discontent.

Not one of God's children can be evil. At worst he is hurt. At worst he attacks others and blames them for his pain. But he is not evil.

Yes, your compassion must go this deep. There is no human being that does not deserve your forgiveness. There is no human being that does not deserve your love.

The Law of Equality

Remember, your good and that of your brother or sister are one and the same. You cannot advance your life by hurting another, nor can you help another by hurting yourself. All attempts to break this simple equation lead to suffering and despair.

Make others equally important. Do not sacrifice for them or ask them to sacrifice for you, but help them when you can and receive their help gratefully when you need it.

More than this is too much. Less than this is too little.

The Law of Reflection

Every time you attack someone else, you reinforce your own guilt. That's why non-violence is so helpful.

You have only one person to forgive in your journey and that is yourself. You are the judge. You are the jury. And you are the prisoner.

※

Conflict is erased from the mind that recognizes its own goodness. Having recognized your goodness, you cannot maintain it except by extending it to others.

How You Interpret Your Experience

How you interpret your experience is rather important. Are you receiving your experience as a blessing or as a punishment? That is the question you must constantly ask yourself.

※

Everything in your experience can be endowed with spiritual qualities by bringing your love, acceptance or forgiveness to it. Even a terminal illness, a rape or a murder can be transformed by the power of your love.

All experience happens for one purpose only: to expand your awareness. Any other meaning you see in your life experience is a meaning that you made up.

When you see the world in its utter neutrality, you will understand that it exists only as a tool for your learning.

Your Brother's Keeper

Whenever you take another person into your heart, you open the door to me as well. There is no person who is not dear to me. For I see into the soul of both the criminal and his victim. I see both calling for love and acceptance, and I will not refuse them. Do not be shocked that I ask the same of you, who are my hands, my feet, and my voice in the world.

To walk with me is to be a servant of God and man simultaneously. You serve man by showing him that God remembers him and cares about him. You bring him food and drink and solace in his suffering. You embrace him and allow him to lay his head on your shoulder. And you encourage him to weep, because he feels abandoned by his parents, his children, his lover, and by God. And as he weeps, you comfort him. For how long has it been since you too felt abandoned and shed gut-wrenching tears of sorrow and regret?

That is the nature of the human experience. It is only appropriate that you should have compassion for your brother. For you share the same experience of suffering and you share the same release.

To honor and care for yourself is your responsibility. Anything that honors you cannot possibly hurt another. But to act in a selfish way, placing your good above another's, invites conflict and resentment.

The ways of the world are harsh in this regard. One who takes advantage of others may be feared but he is not loved. When his fortune changes, which it invariably does, others are more than happy to help pull him down.

⁂

Only by recognizing the worthiness of others is your own worthiness confirmed. When you withhold your love, your enemy is not the only one who is denied that blessing. You are denied it too.

⁂

There is no brother or sister who is unworthy of your love. If you believe that there is one, then your awakening is not complete.

⁂

Having experienced what it is like to hold one person's happiness equally with your own, you can learn to do this with others. You can practice doing unselfish acts for others without expecting anything in return.

When you give without thought of return, the law of grace manifests through you. You become the vehicle through which God's love expresses in this world.

True giving is an overflowing of your love. You don't feel that you are being depleted when you give in this way. In fact, you feel energized, because the love you give away returns to you through the gratitude of others whom you have touched.

Loving Your Enemy

Usually, your fear triggers the fear of others and their fear triggers yours. Often you think such people are blocking your access to the love you want. In fact, they are the doorways to the love that you want.

Your enemy is your ally in disguise. If you offer your enemy love, you will make peace not only with him or her, but with yourself as well.

It is easy for you to love your friend. Most of the time your friend agrees with you and supports you. So it is not hard to love him.

But your enemy disagrees with you. He believes that you are wrong. He sees your weaknesses and does his best to exploit them. If you have a blind spot, you can be sure he sees it.

Your enemy reflects back to you everything that you do not like about yourself. He shows you exactly where your fears and insecurities lie. Only one who opposes you thus can be such an effective teacher.

When you learn to love your enemy, you demonstrate your willingness to look at all of the dark places within your mind. Your enemy is a mirror into which you look until the angry face that you see smiles back at you.

Peace does not come through the agreement of egos, for it is impossible for egos to agree. Peace comes when love and mutual respect are present.

Then, your enemy becomes like a friend who is not afraid to disagree with you. You do not cast her out of your heart just because she sees things differently from you. You listen carefully to what she has to say.

The cause of human conflict is simple: one person dehumanizes another. One side sees the other side as unworthy. As long as people who disagree perceive each other this way, even the simplest details cannot be negotiated. But let each person bring to the other the attitude of respect and acceptance, and even difficult details can be resolved.

Standing Up for Yourself in a Loving Way

Attack happens because you dehumanize the object of your attack. While I encourage you to take issue with actions that are uncaring, hurtful, or disrespectful to you or others, I ask you to do so in a loving way. Do so in a way that respects the people whose actions you oppose. For they are your brothers and sisters too.

Your brother only wants your love, but he does not know how to ask for it. Indeed, he is confused about what love is. So he asks for money, or sex, or something else. He tries to manipulate you to get what he wants.

Of course, you don't want to be manipulated. So you say "no" to his demands, but you do not cast him out of your heart. You do not judge him, or separate from him. You offer him love in response to his fearful thoughts.

You say: "No, friend, I cannot give you what you ask, but I will find a way to support you that affirms both of us. I will not reject you. I will not pretend that you are less worthy than I am. Your need for love is as important as mine and I honor it."

This is how the lover talks to the beloved. He does not say, "I will do anything you want." He says, "I will find a way to honor us both." The lover is equal to the beloved. They are the mutual expression of love.

Loving the Criminal

Your brother has been wounded deeply. He has grown up without a father. He has been addicted to drugs since he was nine years old. And he has lived in a ghetto where he has never felt safe. Do you not feel some compassion for the wounded boy in the man who commits the crime?

If you were to step into his shoes, would you do that much better? Be honest, my friend. And in that honesty, you will find compassion, if not for the man, for the boy who became the man.

And I will tell you right now it is not the man who pulls the trigger, but the boy. It is the boy who is overwhelmed and scared. It is the little one who does not feel loved and accepted. It is the wounded boy who strikes out, not the man.

Do not let your sight be distorted by the angry, disdainful face of the man. Beneath that hard exterior is overwhelming pain and self judgment. Beneath the mask of mismanaged manhood and vicious anger is the boy who does not believe he is lovable.

If you cannot embrace the boy in him, how can you embrace the boy or the girl in yourself? For his fear and yours are not so different.

Criminals are just one group of untouchables in your

society. You do not want to look at their lives. You do not want to hear about their pain.

It is hard for society to look at the pain of its outcasts. But this must be done. If you don't work intentionally with the criminal to help him come to love and accept himself, he will re-enter society with the same anger and vindictiveness.

Building more prisons or putting more police on the streets will not make your neighborhoods safer. These actions just exacerbate the situation by raising the level of fear.

If you want to help, bring the work of forgiveness into the prisons and the neighborhoods. Hire more teachers and counselors and social workers. Feed people, challenge them emotionally and mentally. Offer them experiences of safe emotional bonding. Provide them with opportunities for education and training. Give them hope. Give them acceptance. Give them love.

Those who strike out at others feel that they have no choice. This is the key. Show a man the choices he has and he will not commit a crime.

The lepers of your society are no different than the lepers of my time. They bear everyone's wounds on their skin. They are bold witnesses to the pain you do not want to deal with. Society should be grateful to them, for they are wayshowers. They point to the path of healing all human beings must take.

If you want to change the criminal, you must stop punishing him and begin to love him. Nothing else will work.

Love is not a reward for his trespass. It is the redeemer of his soul. It recalls him to himself. It shifts him out of the reactive cycle in which he dehumanizes himself and others. In the face of genuine love and caring, even the most vicious criminal softens.

You cannot stop hate by fighting it with revenge. Every act of violence begets a counter-act. The only approach that can bring freedom from violence is one that is itself free of violence. Only a spiritual solution works.

To oppose or argue with a false idea is to strengthen it. That is the way of violence. My way is nonviolent. It demonstrates the answer in its approach to the problem. It brings love, not attack, to the ones in pain. Its means are consistent with its ends.

"How do you deal with people who cause suffering for others?" You ask them to be responsible for their actions, but you don't reinforce their guilt.

You tell them that they are mistaken about who they are. Others are mistaken too. Those who abused, neglected, or humiliated them did not know who they were. But you know. And you are willing to treat them in a respectful way and help them rebuild their lives.

If you want someone to act in a loving way, you must be willing to love him. Only your love for him will teach him the meaning of love.

An open heart invites the beloved in. It invites the stranger in, and yes, even the criminal. An open heart is a sanctuary where all are welcome. It is a temple where the laws of Spirit are practiced and celebrated. It is the church you must enter again and again to find redemption.

Crucifixion happens when your heart closes to your brother. Resurrection happens when you open your heart to him, when you stop blaming him for your problems and punishing him for his mistakes, when you learn to love him as you love yourself. Only this will bring release from the prison of fear. Only this!

When you learn to respond to the fears of others in a loving way, you can be sure that your own fears rest in the most compassionate embrace. You are no longer emotionally reactive or ambivalent, but patient and steady, knowing that only love is real. Everything else is illusion.

Love Without Conditions

If loving others is based on agreeing with them, there will be very few people you can love. Fortunately, love runs deeper than that.

When you love without conditions, you support the freedom of others to choose their own way, even when you disagree with them. You trust them to make the best choice for themselves. You trust God's plan for their awakening. You know that they can never make a mistake that will cut them off from God's love or from yours.

Love is the only miracle. All other "miracles" are frosting on the cake. Look beneath the surface of every one of them and you will see a shift from fear to love, from self-protection to self-expansion, from judgment of others to acceptance of them.

Love says: "I accept you as you are. I consider your good equally with my own." Do you have any idea how powerful this statement is? To every person you address in this way, you offer freedom from suffering. And by offering it to him, you offer it to yourself.

Heart to Heart

The Path of Relationship

Relationships offer you a profound spiritual path. Your partner is not only your friend, your lover, and your companion, but also your teacher. S/he reflects back to you all the beauty that lies within you, as well as all the fear, doubt and ambivalence that lies buried deeply within your soul. There is perhaps no more rapid path to psychological wholeness and spiritual awakening than the path of relationship. Yet you must be realistic if you choose to walk this path. While your partnership may occasionally be fun and free of pain - and this is a great goal to aspire to—there may be just as many times when one or both of you is wounded and defensive. Your great accomplishment as a couple is not your ability to navigate around your pain, but your ability to move through your pain together without making the other person responsible for it.

If you can do this work of inner and outer reconciliation, while still holding onto your joy and mutual reverence, you will build a union which is strong and deep. This is the ground love must be anchored in to grow its brightest flower.

The truth is that you can be only as happy with another person as you can be with yourself. If you like who you are, being with your partner can be an extension of your happiness. But, if you do not like yourself, being with your partner can only exacerbate your unhappiness.

Your decision to enter into partnership should not be based on a desire to avoid looking at yourself, but on a willingness to intensify that process. When you live with other people, you are likely to trigger their unhealed wounds and they are likely to trigger yours.

Becoming aware of the unhealed parts of yourself is neither pleasant nor easy. However, it is a necessary part of the journey to psychic wholeness.

While you may be able to avoid looking at the unconscious aspects of your psyche while living alone, you won't be able to avoid looking at them when you are in relationship. Relationship is like a giant backhoe. It digs down through the superficial layers of consciousness and exposes your deepest fears and insecurities.

If you aren't willing to look this deeply, you might

want to question your desire to be in an intimate relationship. You can't get close to another person without coming face to face with yourself.

Relationship is never a panacea for the wounds and traumas of the individual psyche. At best, it is an incubation chamber.

Self Betrayal

There is a tendency when you go into relationship to "go limp," the way an animal goes limp when it is caught by a predator. There is a kind of "false surrender," a giving away of your power to the other person.

The emotional high of a new relationship promises more than it can ever deliver. If you experience "falling in love," you can be sure that you will experience "falling out of love." The very expression "falling in love" should tell you that this experience is about self-betrayal.

In what other area of life would you allow yourself "to

fall" and be whimsical about it? The whole romantic tradition suggests a socially acceptable, nearly institutionalized, form of self-betrayal.

Live with someone before you have learned to live with yourself and you will make a mockery of relationship. Only when you know and accept yourself can you find equality with another.

Unless you commit to loving yourself, others can offer you only detours, side-trips, running in place. Time goes by, but nothing changes. The pain doesn't lift. The pattern of self-betrayal remains.

Do not become lost in the world before you know who you are or your chances of waking up are not strong. The world will be only too happy to give you a role and a responsibility. Other people will be only too happy to assign you a role in their drama.

Establishing in Yourself

If you want to dance with another, root yourself first. Learn to hear your own guidance. Dialogue with the hurt child and the divine host within. Practice forgiveness and compassion for yourself. Be with your experience and learn from it.

Stay in the rhythm of your life. Be open to others, but do not go out of your way to find them. Those who know how to dance will meet you half way. It will not be a struggle.

Inappropriate relationships exacerbate the abuse patterns of the past. Learning is often painful. A better choice can and should be made. But in order to make that choice, you must be able to ask for what you want. If you let another dictate the terms of the relationship, don't be surprised if you remain stuck in a situation that does not honor you.

You know what feels good to you and what does not. Say what you need, speak your truth, and be firm in your commitment to your own healing. Only through your commitment to honor yourself can you attract a partner willing to do the same.

Most relationships fall apart as soon as people reveal themselves. The promise "to have and to hold, in sickness and in health" is for most people an exercise in absurdity, for many people go to the altar without having taken the time to get to know each other.

For this reason, couples should live together successfully for three years before considering marriage. Many relationships will not survive this three-year period of mutual exploration.

Choosing a Partner

Remember, the person who stands before you is not always who s/he seems. The knight in shining armor may be an insecure abuser in disguise and the one offering comfort and support may be a wolf in sheep's clothing.

Always look beyond appearances. Many will come to you claiming to be the one you asked for, but only one will be authentic. Usually, it won't be the one who comes with lots of smoke and mirrors. More often than not, it will be the simple unassuming one, the one who doesn't use big words or promise great gifts, but who takes your hand and looks into your eyes without fear.

Choose your partner well. If you choose one who dances too slowly, you may be held back. If you choose one who dances too fast, you may break your ankle trying to keep up with him or her.

Find a partner who dances at the same speed that you do, one who will complement you and help you realize your potential. Find a partner whom you can empower and assist. Then, you can be together without struggle and your relationship will be mutually beneficial.

Sharing and Boundaries

In a healthy relationship, people are not enmeshed in each other's creative process. Even when they work together, they find a way to support each other's autonomy. Unless you and your partner have this autonomy and the time and space to grow, you won't command each other's respect.

However, autonomy is only one ingredient. Equally important is a shared vision. You and your partner must have dreams, values, and aspirations that you hold in common. You must have a vision of a shared life in which you move together as a couple.

When either the autonomy or the shared vision of the partnership is weak, the relationship cannot prosper. When there isn't enough autonomy, you and your partner are not challenged to grow. When shared vision is weak, your emotional connection with your partner becomes attenuated and you lose sight of your reason for being together.

Neither of these extremes is helpful. You and your partner need to express yourselves both as a couple and as individuals. In a healthy partnership, the commitment to self and the commitment to the relationship are equal in depth and intensity.

It is tragic when two people stay together without individuating. It is equally tragic when people stay together without ever creating a shared purpose.

One should not have to sacrifice becoming an authentic person in order to create a shared purpose with another. Nor should one have to sacrifice creating a shared reality in order to pursue one's own creative potential. These are not mutually exclusive propositions. They are inclusive and contemporaneous ones. Much of the tension and therefore challenge in relationship lies in the attempt to honor and balance these equally important commitments.

The Fear of Intimacy

People who are afraid of love ask for it nonetheless. Yet when it comes to them, they are unable to receive it. They want love to come in a perfect shape and size. And it never comes that way.

People who are afraid of love are ambivalent about giving and receiving. When you are aloof, they feel safe and desire your presence. But when you come close, they get scared and ask you to back off or go away. This emotionally teasing behavior enables them to be in relationship while avoiding intimacy and commitment.

Your job is not to judge these people, analyze them or try to fix them. Accept them as they are. Send them love. But don't live with them or be their partner.

If you are drawn into such a relationship, you must face the fact that you too may be afraid to receive love. Why else would you choose a partner who cannot give it?

Spiritual Marriage

Contrary to popular belief, marriage is not a tie that binds but one that releases. You want the greatest happiness for your partner in the same way that you want the greatest happiness for yourself. You love your partner as you love yourself, with an equal love.

Your partner's needs are as important as your own. Not more important. Not less important. But equally important.

Marriage is not a promise to be together throughout all eternity, for no one can promise that. It is a promise to be present "now." It is a vow that must be renewed in each moment if it is to have meaning.

Infidelity

Adulterous affairs are just the unfortunate outcome of a lack of intimacy between partners. They are not the problem, but the symptom of the problem.

Tending Your Garden

No partner is happy all of the time. Don't allow your happiness to be dependent on your partner's happiness. That will just drag both of you down. Tend to your own garden, and offer your partner a rose to smell. Refusing to tend your garden and complaining that your partner never gives you roses will not make either one of you feel better.

When one person is cranky or sad, the other must dig deeply inside to find the source of love. When she finds the light within, she must carry it for both people for a while. That way the other person does not forget that the light is there, even if he can't see it in himself.

This does not mean that one person should do all the supporting. Relationships require a give and take. But it does mean that there will be times when each partner will have to rise to the occasion and maintain the connection to Source in the face of the other person's fear and mistrust. That is never an easy thing to do. But it is often necessary in the course of a committed relationship.

Validation and Invalidation

As soon as you and your partner feel separate from each other, correction is needed. It's time to stop, take a deep breath, step back and look at what's happening.

Don't blame yourself or the other person. Don't try to be right or make the other person wrong. Just acknowledge the separation you feel and agree together that this separation cannot be bridged while fear is coming up for both of you.

Take some time alone and get clear about what you are afraid of, what you feel you need to defend, what your hurt or anger is about. And try to tune into what positive reassurance or affirmation you need from your partner. Then, when you are both feeling peaceful, take turns asking each other directly for the desired validation.

Almost all fear, anger, and hurt stem from the fact that you're feeling unloved or unappreciated. When someone acts in a way that triggers you, you usually interpret that behavior as meaning that the person doesn't care. Then, if you react in a hurt or angry way, the other person feels invalidated by you. S/he feels that you don't care either.

When you and your partner have difficulty validating each other, the relationship goes into crisis. Negative patterns are set into motion which destroy the trust and block the love you have for each other.

You need to catch this downward spiral before it goes out of control. Take some time out from the relationship to center yourself and get some perspective about what the relationship means to you. Come back into your heart. Then approach the other person.

Don't blame your partner. Just ask respectfully for the validation you need. Don't defend yourself. Just give your partner the validation s/he needs.

When love is present in a relationship, the question is always "What are we going to do?" not "What am I going to do?" Both people want what is best for the relationship, what keeps them connected to love. Finding that shared reality is both the challenge and the reward of every committed relationship. In the process, people grow beyond narrow self-interest and learn to serve the higher purpose of their union.

Forgiveness

Your relationship inevitably asks you to grow in wisdom and emotional strength. Since there are no perfect partners out there, your challenge is to accept and honor the imperfect one who stands before you.

No matter how good your relationship is, you and your partner will forget to honor each other. You will get stressed out and project your pain onto each other. You will attack and defend, give and receive guilt, and generally make a mess of things.

If you and your partner can forgive each other's transgressions and reestablish your trust in one another, then you can deepen in your love and your capacity for intimacy. This is the challenging part of relationship.

Forgiveness is the key to success in every relationship. Indeed, if you and another person are committed to practicing forgiveness, you can live together successfully, even if you don't have a lot in common.

On the other hand, if the two of you are not willing to practice forgiveness, then nothing you try will work. No, not religion, or psychotherapy, or relationship workshops.

Through the practice of forgiveness, imperfect people

become whole, and broken relationships are healed and strengthened. You learn what real love and real essence are all about.

Parental Wounds

The fears that come up for you and your partner do not just stem from your interactions with each other. They are rooted in the unconscious wounds of childhood. Your compulsive behaviors and those of your partner are learned at a very young age in reaction to the conditional love of your parents.

When you come to peace with your parents and accept them as equals, you no longer wish to change to meet their expectations, nor do you want them to change to meet yours. Then, you stop creating parental lessons in your intimate relationships. If you are a man, you stop finding your mother in your wife and trying to be her husband. If you are a woman, you stop finding your father in your husband and trying to be his wife.

The Father and Mother of Creation ask only for what contributes to your awakening. Their love for you is both gentle and fierce. One type of love is not enough. The love of both Father and Mother is necessary.

Father's love teaches courage; Mother's love teaches gentleness. With courage, you walk through your fears. With gentleness, you open your heart.

Problems with the Father translate as an inability to understand and fulfill your creative life purpose. Problems with the Mother translate as an inability to develop loving, intimate, relationships.

When there is lack of learning on one side of the equation, there is usually overcompensation on the other. Balance can be restored only by learning the lesson brought by the more challenging parent.

Soul Mates

The soul-mate cannot manifest until there is honesty and clarity in all of your relationships. You cannot find the soul-mate by abandoning any other human being. You must be right with all of your relationships.

The Beloved

If your life is anchored in the truth of your experience, then that truth can be shared. But if you are looking for truth, or love, or salvation outside yourself, you will be disappointed again and again.

Only by honoring yourself does the beloved come. Those who twist themselves into pretzels in the search for love simply push the beloved away.

Who is the beloved after all? S/He is just the mirror of your own commitment to truth.

Once you meet the beloved in form, your life cannot continue on as it was. All that is separately held must be released. Only what is held together in mutual honoring and embrace can be carried forward. The isolated self must die. The self as partner, as life mate, must be born.

Love is Eternal

You come into relationship to each other in different ways: as children, parents, siblings, friends, workmates, teachers, students. What is important is not the form of the relationship, but the love that abides within the form.

Relationships constantly change form. Children grow up and become parents; parents surrender their bodies to the next adventure; friends move apart; lovers break up; and so it goes. No form remains the same.

Growth must continue. Forms must come and go. That is the bittersweet quality of life. If you become attached to the form or throw away the love just because the form is changing, you will suffer unnecessarily. The challenge is to let the form go, but hold onto the love.

Love is eternal. It is limitless. It cannot be defined by time or space.

Love continues to be Itself. It does not change. The form love takes may change, but love itself does not change.

Too often you deny the love you have for each other when the form changes. That is just another kind of attachment to form. It says: "I must have love in this particular way or I do not want it at all." That is childish. When you grow up, you realize that you can't always have things exactly the way you want them, especially when other people are involved.

Ending an Agreement

When one person no longer wants to keep an agreement, the agreement is off. You can't hold another person against his or her will. If you try to do so, you will push love away.

Love survives the ending of agreements, if you will allow it to. If you won't, you only cheat yourself.

If you decide to separate, please do so in a loving way, without holding onto resentments or grievances. It is not easy when a relationship ends or changes form, and gentleness on both sides is extremely important if healing is to happen for both people.

Be grateful for what you have learned and experienced together. Be cognizant of the issues that separated you and take responsibility for your part in them. When you begin another relationship, be aware when similar issues arise and see if you can deal with these issues in a more generous and responsible way.

Love and freedom go hand in hand. Love cannot be contained forever in a specific form. It must break free of all forms, all conditions, if it is to become itself fully.

Grant to the other person the freedom to be who s/he is and the form will take care of itself. Try to take away that freedom and the form will become a prison for both of you.

The Freedom to Love

Love and freedom are inseparable. You cannot love if you do not have a choice. All forms of bondage are assaults not just on freedom, but on love itself, because love cannot exist when you lose the freedom to choose.

The great tragedy of love is not that you may choose not to be with your partner. That is sad perhaps, but not tragic. The real tragedy is that you and your partner may stay together or separate because you believe that you have no other choice.

If there is love, there must be the freedom to choose. To give and receive this freedom takes courage. It takes heart. It takes patience. But that is the nature of love. And those who love each other through all the conditions, all the ups and downs of life, all the forms though which love expresses are patient and courageous beyond measure.

Your experience of love will be diminished in direct proportion to your need to control it. Control places conditions upon that which must be without conditions. When you establish conditions on love, you experience the conditions, not the love. You encounter the form, not the content.

Divorce

Relationships ultimately end themselves. The energy and interest is simply not there anymore. The road to divorce begins with the recognition that there is no longer a shared purpose and a mutual energetic attraction.

Not all relationships are meant to be marriages. Some are temporary learning experiences lasting a few months or a few years. Unfortunately, people marry before they know in their hearts they have found a lifetime partner. But, as long as the mistake is mutually acknowledged, no harm is done.

Shame about making a mistake in marriage does not serve anyone. Lots of people make these mistakes. Some people suffer with their mistakes, staying in relationships long after they have lost their sacredness. Others bail out of their relationships too soon, before they have learned their lessons and come to completion with their partners. This is not a new story.

Divorce, like marriage, begins first in the hearts of the partners. It is an organic process of dis-entanglement. When people have gone as far together as they are capable of or willing to go, divorce is the only humane solution. It is unethical to try to hold another person against his or her will.

At best, the divorce happens in the context of gratitude toward the partner for the time shared. As such, it is not only a separation, but also a completion.

It would be dishonest to suggest that children are not wounded by the divorce of their parents. On the other hand, they are also wounded by the unwillingness of their parents to love and respect each other.

If the detachment of divorce helps the partners to come back into mutual respect, then it can be progressive for the children. Children benefit whenever they see adults acting in a loving and respectful manner to one another.

However, in a healing divorce situation, parents must focus intently on providing consistent attention to the children so that they do not feel abandoned or to blame. The importance of this cannot be overemphasized.

True detachment comes from familiarity with others, not from estrangement. Distancing others does not bring detachment, but its opposite. Only when you let others into your heart do you become capable of releasing them.

No relationship lasts forever. People come together because they have important things to learn together. When those lessons are learned, they move on to other challenges with other teachers. That is how it is.

The key is not to worry about how long a relationship lasts, but to give it your best energy and attention. Experience as much joy as you can with your partner. Learn as much as you can from the painful times. Do your best to be honest and clear with each other. Stretch your comfort zones a little. Be flexible and constructive. Be the first to yield and to bless. Give without worrying about what you are going to get back. And when you fall down, get back up and laugh at your own stupidity.

You will never be perfect in your ability to give or receive love. Don't try to be. Just try to be a little more open to give and receive love than you were before.

Promise and Fulfillment

Relationships are a two-edged sword. They promise bliss, yet bring up the most primitive, unintegrated emotions. They promise companionship, yet challenge you to deal with seemingly irreconcilable differences. They promise an end to loneliness, yet open the door to a deeper aloneness.

No other area of your life offers you as many opportunities to understand your wounds and heal them. Your partner is the mid-wife to your birth into your full potential. Thanks to him or her, you learn to surrender the dysfunctional patterns that compromise your happiness. Through the mirror your partner holds up to you, you discover your wholeness and learn to give your gift to the world.

Real Love

When you have learned to consider another person's good equally with your own, you become capable of doing it with all people. Then, no one is excluded from your love. What you give to one, you give to all. What you receive from one, you receive from all.

Real Love is the end of separate thoughts, separate agendas, separate wills. It has one thought, one agenda, one will, one love for all beings. But none of this will mean anything to you until you learn to love one person as you love yourself. For most of you, this is the doorway you will open to divine bliss.

Giving the Gift

Your Life is a Work of Art

Your life is a work of art and you need to be busy about it even as a bee is busy pollinating flowers. And remember, work that is not joyful to you accomplishes nothing of value in the world.

There are no failures on this planet. Even the homeless, the prostitutes, the drug dealers, are molding the clay that was given to them.

Because you do not like a particular piece of artwork does not mean that it ceases to be a work of art. There are no boring stories out there. Each tale is a gem. Each sculpture has genius.

You cannot say that what one person builds with his life is less valuable than what another person builds. All you can say in truth is that you prefer what one person has built to what another has built. You have your preferences.

Fortunately God does not share them. Not yours or anyone else's. God listens to everyone's story. Her ear is to each person's heart.

Embracing the Gift

Whatever gift you have to give is the perfect one. It does not matter if it is not the one you thought you would have or the one you wanted.

When you embrace the gift, the purpose of your life reveals itself. You see how every lesson, every problem, every moment of suffering was absolutely necessary for the gift to be given and received.

God does not give questionable gifts.

Often you will not know the meaning of the gift until the gift is put to work in your life. That can be frustrating, but it is inevitable.

The gifts of God do not feed your ego expectations. Their value is of a higher order. They help you open to your true nature and purpose here. Sometimes they seem to close a door and you don't understand why. Only when the right door opens do you understand why the wrong door was closed.

What you deeply value has your full, loving attention. It is nurtured, watered, and brought into fullness and truth. It does not happen overnight. It does not happen exactly how or when you want it to. It flourishes through your commitment, your constancy, your devotion. What you love prospers. If unfolds. It gets roots and wings. This is the movement of grace in your life.

The gifts you have been given in this life do not belong to you alone. They belong to everyone. Do not be selfish and withhold them.

Don't imprison yourself in a lifestyle that holds your spirit hostage and provides no spontaneity or grace in your life. Risk being yourself fully.

Let go of the expectations others have for you and get in touch with what brings you the greatest joy and fulfillment. Live from the inside out, not from the outside in.

To move toward your joy is not selfish. It is in fact the most generous action you can take. That is because your gift is needed. The spirit of others cannot be lifted up unless you trust your gift and give it to the world.

Consider how empty life would be if others around you chose to abandon their gifts. All that you find wonderful in life—the music, the poetry, the films, the sports, the laughter—would vanish if others withheld their gifts from you.

Do not withhold your gift from others. Do not make the mistake of thinking that you have no gift to give. Everyone has a gift.

Your gift brings joy to yourself and joy to others. It is a creative expression that breaks down the barriers of separation and allows others to know who you are.

Appreciation

Only that which comes from your heart with great enthusiasm will prosper on all levels. Only that which you love will touch others and bring true appreciation your way. Appreciation is the natural, spontaneous flow of energy back to you when others feel connected to you and your story. There is nothing you can do to precipitate appreciation other than to be yourself and tell the truth.

Many of your gifts go unacknowledged because they don't match your pictures of what a gift should be. Often, you devalue your gift by comparing it to that of others, or you place a condition on your willingness to offer the gift.

You say "I will sing only if I have an audience of 1,000 people and I make at least $5,000!" Supposing not that many people have heard of you, how many offers to sing are going to come your way?

This is self-defeating. How is your lifework to evolve if you do not take the first step to bring it into existence?

No matter how anxious you are to grow up with your gift, you must first take the time to nurture and develop it. Find a good teacher. Sing for your friends and family members. Take small risks, then bigger ones. Gradually, you will gain skill and confidence. Then, without doing anything, the audiences will grow.

Those who refuse to start small never accomplish anything. They shoot for the moon and never learn to stand on the earth.

The way you relate to your gift says a lot about

whether you are happy or not. Happy people are expressing their gifts on whatever level and in whatever arena life offers them. Unhappy people are holding onto their gifts until life gives them the perfect venue.

Part of trusting the gift is letting go of the way you think the gift should be received. That is not your affair. It is none of your business. No matter how great you become, you will never know who will be touched by your work and who will turn away.

To give the gift, you must release it. You must not be attached to who receives it and who doesn't.

You can't hold onto your gift and give it away at the same time. When you see the absurdity of trying to do this, you will give your gift the wings it deserves.

Authenticity

If you are true to yourself, you will neither conform to the expectations of others nor will you isolate yourself from their feedback.

The desire for approval prevents honest self-expression. It is soft and apologetic. The need to shock or offend others prevents dialogue and intimacy. It pushes people away.

Authentic expression is neither offensive nor apologetic. It tells its truth and invites dialogue. It builds bridges of understanding between people.

As you embrace your gift and move through your fear of expressing it, old, self-limiting lifestyle structures are de-energized. Without receiving new energy, these structures crumble and fall apart.

Your work situation, your family life, your sleeping and eating patterns all begin to shift as you get about the business of honoring yourself and moving toward your joy. You detach from roles and relationships that no longer serve your continued growth. This happens spontaneously, without forcing or violation.

When faced with your absolute, uncompromising commitment to yourself, others either join you or move swiftly out of your way. Grey spaces created by your ambivalence—your desire to have something and give it up at the same time—move toward yea or nay. Clarity emerges as the clouds of self-doubt and attachment are burned away by the committed, radiant Self.

When one person moves toward individuation, it gives everyone permission to do the same. Dysfunctional family structures are dismantled and new structures that honor the individuals involved are put in their place.

This is what commitment to Self does. It destroys sloppiness, co-dependency, neurotic bargaining for love, boredom, apathy and critical behavior. It empowers individuals to be authentic and responsible for their choices in life.

One person's fidelity to Self and willingness to live her dream explodes the entire edifice of fear that surrounds her. It is that simple. And it all happens as gently as the first "yes" said in the silence of the heart.

In the World but not of It

If your work is not joyous, if it doesn't express your unique talents and abilities, and if it doesn't uplift others, it is not spiritual work. It is the world's work.

I have asked you to be in the world but not of it. What does this mean?

It means that you choose work that you can do joyfully in the spirit of love. That way your labor becomes a gift.

If there is sacrifice involved, there will be no joy. And so there will be no gift.

Only work that is joyful will bring you happiness. Only work that is joyful will bring happiness to others. The means must be consistent with the ends.

Be wary of work motivated by guilt, fear or spiritual pride. Do not try to save yourself by helping others. Do not try to save others when it is you yourself who needs to be saved.

Do not cheat yourself by working out of sacrifice. Do not cheat others by working out of greed. Do not deny yourself what you need to live with dignity. Do not take more than you need. Material wealth will not bring you happiness.

Having found your lifework, the greatest obstacle to its fulfillment lies in your attempt to "direct" it. You cannot make your spiritual work happen. If you try, you will fail.

Spiritual work requires surrender. Worldly work requires the illusion of control.

As soon as you give up the need to control, any work can become spiritual. As soon as you try to take charge, the most spiritual projects begin to fall apart.

Spiritual Rewards

There is no more truth in the religion of abundance than there is in the religion of sacrifice. God does not necessarily reward spiritual work with material success. All rewards are spiritual. Happiness, joy, compassion, peace, sensitivity: these are the rewards for a life lived in integrity.

You must learn, once and for all, to stop measuring spiritual riches with a worldly yardstick.

If material success comes, it is often a test to see if you can transcend self-interest and greed. Material wealth, like all other gifts, is given that it may be shared with others.

Don't make the mistake of thinking that your lifework must bring in a large paycheck. On the other hand, don't make the mistake of thinking that you must be poor to serve God. A rich person can serve God as well as one of humble means if he is willing to share his riches. It matters not how much you hold in your hands, but whether your hands are extended outward to your brother or sister.

Commitment

Having a goal means nothing if you are not committed to it. If you are not willing to put the full force of your being behind that goal, then your dreams are not going to become reality.

When you get really honest with yourself, you know that no one else is preventing you from realizing your goals. You are the only person who can sabotage your dreams.

You bring into your life what you allow to come in. If you say "no" to what you don't want, you bring in what you do want. It is that simple.

The only factor that makes all this complicated is that you don't always know what you want or, if you do, you don't trust it and remain committed to it. When your unconscious desires are different from your conscious goals, what you bring into your life reflects a mixture of both.

That is why the time you take to integrate and unify the different needs and wants of your psyche is time well spent. When there is un-conflicted desire in the heart and clarity on all levels of consciousness, the creative process flows easily.

Co-Creation

All creation is really co-creation. You determine what you want, commit to it, and move toward it, and the opportunities you need to realize your goal come your way. To be sure, you must keep surrendering your expectations. You must be open to the opportunities that arise, but you do not have to make them happen.

One of the great "Ahahs" on the spiritual path is the recognition that you don't have to make your life happen. It happens by itself.

Remember, you cannot experience joy in life by following or opposing the ideas and actions of other people. You experience joy only by remaining faithful to the truth within your own heart.

The Ministry of Love

See the Light in Others

Do not focus on the darkness, for it is not ultimately real. Focus, instead, on the indwelling goodness of all beings.

By seeing the light in others, you will be constantly baptizing. You will be offering communion. Even as people confess their sins, you will be affirming the Truth within them. Do not focus on what is missing or what needs to be corrected. Focus on what is always there and can never be taken away. Focus on what is right and what is good. Because you do not look for weaknesses, you will help people find their strength. Because you do not look for wounds, you will help people find their gratitude.

Healing

Being a healer means accepting your inherent capacity to be free of conflict, free of guilt, free of judgment or blame. If you accept this capacity in yourself, you will demonstrate miracles in your life just as I did.

Don't try to heal other people. Just heal yourself. Every time you heal a judgmental thought or feeling of separation, every mind and heart in the universe feels it. Your healing belongs not just to you, but to all beings.

The Ministry of Love

When you learn to love yourself, you cannot help loving others. It is not hard to do.

When you love, there is no limit on that love. It constantly recycles, flowing in and out of the heart. Like waves breaking and receding on a beach, the tides of love are steady and dependable. They touch every shoreline with their blessing.

Love is not something you do. Love is who you are. You are the embodiment of love in this moment. Nothing less.

Wherever you go, Love goes with you. Love moves with your legs, reaches with your hands, speaks with your voice, and sees with your eyes.

Because of you, Love is everywhere. Without you, It would be invisible. That is why your service is needed. No, not to preach or proselytize, but to listen, to comfort, to care.

In your silence, Love's presence is felt. In your acceptance, Love's compassion is experienced. In your smile, Love's delight is made manifest.

What expresses through you is the Christ Presence Itself, the very embodiment of God's love. I am not the only Christ.

When I heard the call, I answered it. Now you hear it too and you answer it by following this simple teaching: "whatever is not loving must be forgiven; and what is forgiven becomes love's patient blessing on an imperfect world.

You are all channels through which God's love can flow to others. There is no mystery in this. As soon as you make space for God in your heart, He brings the stranger to your doorstep. As soon as you make space for God in your community, He brings the outcasts and the disenfranchised into the sanctuary of your church.

That is the way of Spirit. When you offer love, those who are in need of that love will find you. They are brought to God through your loving presence.

There was a time when I offered to be the door for you. Now you too must become the door.

The Greatest Teachers

It is a rare person who can go about her work without calling attention to herself, without seeking publicity, without building an organization around her. It is a rare person who inspires without taking credit, who heals without charging a fee and gives without asking anything in return.

The greatest teachers are the most humble, the most loving, the most empowering to others. If you wish to find such a teacher, you must look beyond appearances. Find the man or woman who promises you nothing, but loves you without hesitation. Find the teacher who makes no pretension to fix or to teach, yet who opens your heart when s/he looks into your eyes.

⁂

There is only one question an authentic teacher can ask you: "Are you happy right now?" If the answer is "yes," then you are already in heaven. If the answer is "no," then s/he asks "why not?"

You may give the teacher thirty pages of testimony as to why you are unhappy, but s/he will simply ask again "why not?" And sooner or later, you will realize that all your reasons for not being happy are about the past.

All a teacher can do is ask "Why not now?" S/he is not interested in your past or future.

⁂

No one can resist a person who radiates love. Everyone comes to sit at his feet. Can you imagine that? People are not even invited, never mind proselytized, yet they come anyway. They come because love calls to them and they respond.

You do not have to go out aggressively to spread the message. You do not have to hit people over the head with it and drag them back to your churches or synagogues. Just love each other, and people will come. They will come and fill themselves to the brim, and they will return home with their cup running over. That is the way this teaching spreads.

Being a minister of love is effortless. You just keep loving, and people keep coming. You keep admitting your mistakes and confessing your worries and fears, and people hold you ever more deeply in their hearts.

Religion

I hate to disappoint you, but the truth is that no one needs religion. You don't need to hold onto the husk. But you do need to break it open and plant the seed.

Dig deeply enough in the garden of your faith and you will find the voices of truth that will help you open your heart to love's presence. And that is where you must focus. That is where you must plant the seed of faith that will take root in your life.

There are many beautiful trees that flower in the springtime. One is not better than another. Each has its special beauty. Seen together, they make an extraordinary garden. So it is with approaches to the divine. Each approach has its own beauty and integrity. It speaks to certain people and not to others. That is the way it should be. One tree is not better than another. One religion is not better than another.

Regardless of the tradition you belong to, you must find the seed, separate it from the husk, and see that it is planted in your lifetime. You must find the core teaching that connects you to love and pass that teaching on to your children. That is the only way that a tradition stays healthy.

A barren tree will make no fruit. A religion that does not help its followers connect to love will not prosper.

Anyone can create a religion for insiders and exclude those who would challenge his beliefs. This has nothing to do with spirituality. It has more to do with the insecurities of the individual.

Cults thrive on this kind of insecurity. In the name of spiritual surrender, initiates are asked to capitulate to the authority structure of the cult. In this way, brainwashing poses as enlightenment.

Hierarchical, closed belief systems promise Shangri-La and deliver Alcatraz. They offer freedom from suffering and deliver physical abuse and mind control. You can't prevent people from being drawn into such situations, but you can offer them a helping hand when they are ready to get out.

New Skins for New Wine

Tolerance for differences is essential to the creation of a safe, loving space. It is not necessary for people to have the same beliefs to experience spiritual communion with one another. Communion happens through the extension of love and non-judgment. It can happen anywhere, with any group of people, if they are committed to loving and respecting one another.

The time has come for churches and temples to redefine themselves. They must cease to be places where minds cling to linear beliefs in fearful agreement, and become places of self-exploration, where differences are welcome. Love, not agreement, must become the bond that holds the community together.

A society that tolerates differences of perspective is a society that is based on the practical demonstration of love and equality. Equality between people requires that all ideas be heard and all perspectives be considered. The path to truth has never been an easy one. It certainly has never been one based on expediency.

A Living Church

In a living church, each person is free to determine her own spiritual path. She is granted total freedom in this pursuit, and in return grants this freedom to others. She agrees not to try to convert or to fix anyone else. She asks for unconditional acceptance and support for her journey and gives the same to others in return.

In a living church, power lies in the hands of the congregation. The minister's role is to lead by example and empower others to walk their unique spiritual path. The more successful the minister is in empowering others, the more participatory the organization becomes.

As a skillful facilitator, the minister invites others to take responsibility, to share their gifts, and to co-create the organization with him. When the congregation is fully empowered, the minister's work in that place is complete and he can retire or move on to another environment that will challenge him further.

A living church is a therapeutic, healing community, but without any therapists or healers.

It invites you to get out of the way and trust the Spirit to heal. When you try to become the healer, the minister, the teacher, the technician, you just add more confusion, fear and guilt to everybody's plate.

A living church does not offer techniques for fixing or salvation. It provides a safe space and invites you to share your experience with others. It asks you to help create that safe space by being a gentle witness to others. That is all.

That is enough for a lifetime.

You don't have to have all the answers to grow, to walk through your fears, to inhabit your life more completely. As you tell your story and witness to the stories of others, the alchemical process of transformation begins in your heart.

That process has its own rules, its own integrity, its own time-table. As you learn to trust it, Spirit takes charge of your life and healing and miracles happen as a matter of course.

Open Mind, Open Heart

Genuine community happens only to the extent that it fosters an open mind and an open heart.

You cannot foster an open mind if you teach any dogma. Giving people answers is manipulative and controlling. Instead, help people articulate their questions and begin the search for their own answers.

You cannot foster open-heartedness if you exclude anyone from your community or give preferential treatment to any member. People open their hearts when they feel welcome and treated as equals. Nothing closes the heart down quicker than competition for love and attention.

This is why the primary focus of the community must be on setting clear boundaries and establishing a healthy group process. Each person must be given a chance to be heard and encouraged to communicate in a non-blaming way. When a safe space is created in which feelings can be expressed without attacking others, misunderstandings, judgments and projections can be dissolved. People can return to their hearts. Trust can be reestablished.

※

By confessing your judgments and fears to others, you help establish a group culture that is compassionate and forgiving of mistakes. Neither you nor others have to beat yourselves up when fear or judgment comes up.

When ego is held compassionately, it is no longer held by ego, but by something else more gentle and allowing, something merciful, accepting, forgiving. It doesn't matter what you call it.

Through the practice of voluntary confession, a community of equals is born. No one is more spiritual than anyone else. Each person has judgments and wishes to release them. When one person acknowledges a mistake, the others think "there go I. I am no different than my brother."

There is no pretension to spirituality here, no desire

for perfection or shame about imperfection. There is just acceptance of the ego as it rises and falls. There is patience and compassion. This deepens the safety of the space.

Such a community offers unconditional blessing and forgiveness. It is a safe place where ego rises without condemnation, a sacred space where each contraction, each movement of fear, is gently acknowledged and released. It is a sanctuary where heart and mind close only to open more fully to the presence of love.

Real Love

Real love is unconditional. It does not exclude anyone for any reason. It requires you to see beyond appearances, to see others from an inner conviction that all people carry the divine spark within them.

Real love does not seek to bind, control, or enslave, but to liberate, to empower, to set others free to find their own truth. What church or temple has this for an agenda? What religious structure gives its members the freedom to self-actualize in the name of love?

What church extends love and inclusion to all? What community of human beings is dedicated to seeing beyond its fears and learning to love its enemies?

When I asked for a church, was this not the kind of church I asked for? Did I not ask for a community that would recognize the Christ presence in all human beings, a community where no one would be ostracized or cast out? What is salvation, I ask you, if you do not offer it to everyone, regardless of his appearance or beliefs?

People intuitively understand that if they take up this path, their lives will never be the same. I understand that.

Many people like to play at surrender, while retaining their addiction to control. They want to love others who are like them while retaining their judgments about others who are different. That way, they appear to be spiritual, without having to risk becoming vulnerable. They talk about love, but keep a hard shell around them which pushes love away. They have the semblance of love, but not the real thing. Real love would crack their lives open.

Abundance and Grace

Scarcity Thinking

Scarcity thinking results from your perception that you are not worthy of love. When you do not feel worthy of love, you project lack outside you.

The experience of scarcity is not God punishing you. It is you showing yourself a belief that needs to be corrected.

Abundance comes into your life, not because you have learned to memorize some mumbo jumbo incantation, but because you have learned to bring love to the wounded aspects of your psyche. Love heals all perception of division and lack, restoring the original perception of wholeness, free of sin or guilt.

The Meaning of Abundance

Contrary to popular opinion, abundance does not mean that you have a lot of money or material possessions. Abundance means that you have what you need, use it wisely, and give what you don't need to others. Your life has poise, balance, and integrity. You don't have too little. You don't have too much.

On the other hand, scarcity does not mean that you don't have enough money or material possessions. It means that you don't value what you have, don't use it wisely, or don't share it with others. Scarcity may mean that you have too little. It may also mean that you have too much. Your life is out of balance. You want what you don't have, or you have what you don't want.

I assure you that you will not increase your happiness just by increasing your material possessions. You increase your happiness only by increasing your energy, your self-expression and your love. If that also increases your pocketbook, then so be it. You have more to enjoy and share with others.

The goal in life should not be to accumulate resources that you don't need and cannot possibly use. It should be to earn what you need, enjoy and can share joyfully with others.

The abundant person has no more or less than she can use responsibly and productively. She does not obsess on protecting what she has or in obtaining what she does not need. She is content with what she has, and is open to giving and receiving all the resources that God brings into her life.

The Law of Energy

You can give and receive only what you have, not what you don't have. The attempt to give or receive what you do not have is futile. It can end only in disappointment and sorrow.

If you are loving, you receive love, because love always returns to itself. If you demand love, you receive demands for love. As you sow, so do you reap. The law of energy is circular. What goes out comes back and what comes back goes out.

Giving and receiving are the same thing. Giving is receiving. Receiving is giving. When you know this, the whole chess game falls apart. The mystery is over.

Economic Justice

To give what you have keeps the flow of resources moving. To give less than you have creates an imbalance in the flow of resources.

No one but you can determine what you have to give. That is why no system of economics, no matter how pure, can create a fair distribution of the collective resources of human beings. Only fair people can create a fair economy.

Fairness happens voluntarily. It never happens by control. People have to be free to make mistakes and learn from them. Otherwise, the system is not open and growth is not possible.

Energy and Form

It is the nature of energy to expand. It is the nature of form to contract. This is one of the inevitable paradoxes you must live with.

The energy of creation wants to open you up and the structure of your mind and body resists that expansion. The important thing to realize is that all structure belongs to the past, while energy only exists in the moment.

It is like water that flows by you as you watch from the bank of a river. It is never the same water you are looking at. In the same manner, the energy inside you is never the same energy that it was five minutes ago. It is always new energy.

That is fortunate indeed, because it means that you are never limited to the past. Every adjustment you make in consciousness in the present has an immediate effect on the energy that is able to move through you.

Love opens the mind/body consciousness to its maximum energetic potential, enabling others to "feel" the energy of acceptance, gratitude, and kindness flowing directly to them. This opens their hearts and minds to their own potential and empowers them to share their creative gifts with others. This is how abundance is generated in the world.

Relinquishing the Ego's Agenda

The energy of creation moves through you to others and through others to you. Your alignment with this energy requires the relinquishment of your ego agenda.

Your ego agenda operates from the belief that you can manipulate people and events to obtain the outcome you want. Your ego agenda is selfish and short-sighted. It does not consider the good of others, and therefore it does not consider your ultimate good.

When you cheat someone out of something s/he deserves, you lose not only what you thought you would gain; you also lose what you would have gained if you had acted in a less selfish way. Every attempt to gain in a selfish manner eventually leads to loss and defeat, because selfish actions are not supported by the universal energy.

Those who take advantage of others may seem to gain the upper hand through their great determination and skill, but they do not prevail in the long run. Their victory is a temporary one. Goliath reigns only until David rises up to defeat him. In the end, as I have said, "the meek inherit the earth."

Grace

Grace happens when you abide with what is. Struggle happens when you push what is away or try to bring something else in. Grace happens when you accept. Struggle happens when you reject or try to fix. Grace is natural. Struggle is unnatural. Grace is effortless. Struggle takes great effort. Struggle means that you get in the way. Grace means that you stay out of the way.

Grace is not continuous for anyone. New lessons emerge that must be learned. No matter how far the heart has opened, there will be times when it still contracts in fear. That is to be expected.

Grace comes and goes. Alignment happens and is lost.

God appears and disappears. Self is forgotten and remembered.

Grace happens in the flow of life, not apart from it. And life is always moving, like a river, twisting and turning through the landscape.

It begins as a mountain stream, rushing downward, impetuous and intent to reach its goal. Then it levels out and moves for what seems like an eternity through fields and plains, separating into different streams, joining with other bodies of water. By the time it reaches the ocean, it no longer has any urgency. Instead, it has a confidence born of experience. By the time it reaches the ocean, it no longer sees itself as anything other than ocean. It rests completely in itself, without beginning or end.

It will be that way with you too. When you enter fully into your life, all that held you separate will be gently washed away. Breathing in, you will open to embrace what comes. Breathing out, you will gently release it.

You enter the circle of grace when you offer love to yourself or to another person. You enter the circle of fear when you withhold love from yourself or another.

When you stand inside of one circle, the reality of the other circle comes into question. This is why you often have the sense that there are two mutually exclusive worlds in your experience.

The grateful cannot imagine being unjustly treated. The resentful cannot imagine being loved by God. Which world would you inhabit? It is your choice.

Gratitude is the choice to see the love of God in all things. No being can be miserable who chooses thus. For the choice to appreciate leads to happiness as surely as the choice to depreciate leads to unhappiness and despair.

One gesture supports and uplifts. The other devalues and tears down.

The Dance of Life

If you want to understand what flexibility means watch the behavior of a young sapling in the wind. Its trunk is thin and fragile, yet it has awesome strength and endurance. That is because it moves with the wind, not against it.

When conditions are right for something to happen, it will happen without great effort. When conditions are not right, even great effort will not succeed. Moving with the wind requires a sensitivity to the conditions at hand. There are times to rest and retreat, and times to move energetically forward.

Look at the tree moving in the wind. The tree has deep roots and wide branches. It is fixed below, flexible above. It is a symbol of strength and surrender.

You can develop the same strength of character by moving flexibly with all the situations in your life. Stand tall and be rooted in the moment. Know your needs, but allow them to be met as life knows how. Do not insist that your needs be met in a certain way. If you do, you will offer unnecessary resistance. The trunk of the tree snaps when it tries to stand against the wind.

Move in the wind. Your life is a dance. It is neither good nor bad. It is a movement, a continuum.

Your choice is a simple one. You can dance or not. Deciding not to dance will not remove you from the dance floor. The dance will continue on around you.

Buddha's Window

The Buddha began in the same place where you begin. The nature of suffering does not change. You have not been given a special handicap, nor were you given fewer abilities.

There is no difference between you and Buddha, or between Buddha and me. You are pure being. The Buddha is pure being. You struggle with identification with form. So did the Buddha. So did I.

We are all tested. We all build on quicksand and get sucked down into the muck of conditioned existence. But we are not the conditioned.

All conditions come from us. As soon as we stop placing conditions on our embrace of life, relative existence falls away.

We are the lotus swimming on the murky surface of the pond. We are the awareness, the profound discovery that grows out of the darkness of conditions. We are the white flower, nurtured by those murky waters.

If you are looking for beauty without sadness, you will not find it. If you are looking for celebration without the poignancy of pain, you will search in vain. All that is transcendent comes from the lowly, the light from the dark, the flower from the mud.

Give up your linear thinking, your rigid, left-brain expectations of what spirituality means. Life is not one dimensional. If the absolute is truly absolute, then there is no place where it is not found.

Don't choose one side of the argument. Learn to take both sides and work toward the middle. Both extremes reflect each other. Those who are in conflict share the same lesson.

There is only one way to freedom. Buddha called it The Middle Way, the way between all extremes. You can't get there by taking sides. You can't get there by choosing the good over the bad, or the light over the dark. Your path goes through the place where good and evil cross, where the light is obstructed, casting long shadows.

There are no maps that take you to this place. If you ask one person, he says "go to the right." If you ask another, he says "go to the left."

If you ask the pessimist where you can find truth, he will say "it was here yesterday. You missed it." If you ask the optimist, he will reply: "it will be here tomorrow."

Who gives the correct answer? Is there, in fact, a correct answer? Or is the expectation of a correct answer itself the illusion?

When you can observe the argument without taking sides, when you can be in the middle of the battleground without attacking anyone, then you have arrived in the place where the lotus blooms. Few will notice you, but it will not matter. You have come home. You have slipped through the veil. You are no longer an object blocking the light, but the window that allows the light to stream through.

The Kingdom of Heaven

Essence

Divine Essence is not born and it does not die. It exists before physical birth and after physical death. It is not subject to the highs and lows of mental-emotional experience. It is a steady, loving presence, to which you return when you have stopped crucifying yourself or attacking others.

When you feel unloved, unworthy or cut off from others, you are forgetting your Essence. When you remember your Essence, you remember your Spiritual connection to all Beings.

This has nothing to do with your sex, your race, your economic standing, your nationality or your religion. It has nothing to do with who you think you are or who others think you are.

Divine Essence within you is wholly lovable and loving. When you are in touch with your Essence, you know that you are acceptable exactly as you are. There is nothing about you or anyone else that needs to be improved or fixed. To know your Essence, you must discard your self-judgments and your criticisms of your brother or sister.

Lifting the Veil

When you look outside, you don't find God, because God isn't out there. God is within. God isn't in how life appears. That's just the veil. To see the truth, you must lift the veil.

God isn't the temporal, the changing, the inconstant. God is the eternal, the unchanging, the constant, because God is love and never stops being love.

If you aren't looking for God within your own heart, you can live your whole life and never know that God exists. You can be bitter, resentful, angry. There's nothing to be done about this if you insist on looking outside of yourself for validation or approval.

An about-face is necessary. You must turn to the place where God abides. You must find the place in you which is unconditionally aligned with love.

You can't do this while you are blaming others or holding onto grievances. Nor can you do it when you are feeling guilty and beating yourself up for making mistakes. All judgment of self and other must go. You must come to God empty, with open arms.

The Door to the Divine Presence

The door to the Divine Presence opens through your heart. It opens through your gentle acceptance of yourself in this moment. It opens through your gentle acceptance of others as they are in this moment, through your willingness to be with others without judging them or trying to fix them.

The door to the Divine Presence opens through your simple remembrance of God in this moment. It opens when you no longer need to make reality fit your pictures of how it should be, when you can surrender everything you think you know and come to each moment empty of expectations.

If you want to connect with the Divine Presence, open your heart. Be gentle with yourself and others. See your judgments for what they are: the obstacle to peace within and peace without.

God is not some abstraction, but a living presence in your life. It is the breath that animates all forms, the ultimate inclusive understanding, the quintessential blessing of love on all things.

Do not expect your relationship with God to look like anyone else's or try to measure your spirituality by comparing what happens for you with what happens for others. God's presence in your life is totally unique.

Don't accept concepts of God that come from others or make the mistake of thinking that someone else has more spiritual knowledge than you do. Ignore the priests, psychics, and shamans who would give you answers. They are the blind leading the blind. Anyone who is close to God knows that it is you who gives God permission to be present in your life, only you.

Cultivate your relationship with God directly. Enter the silence of your own heart. Talk to God. Pray and ask for guidance. Open the dialogue and listen for God's answers within and in the signs that She sends into your life.

Get to know God in your own experience. Accept no substitutes. And know absolutely that any message of fear does not come from God or from any of Her ministers.

Do not prescribe for others or let them prescribe for

you. Even your bibles, channeled documents and holy books are someone else's experience. Accept no teaching other than the one of your heart.

Take communion in the silence where you meet God face to face. You, my friend, are enough. You are sufficient. All the jewels of knowledge can be found within your own mind. All the joys of Spirit can be discovered in your own heart.

Gather with others in mutual appreciation and gratitude to God. Meditate and pray together. Break bread together. Give, receive, serve together, but do not take direction from one another. Instead, honor each other's experience. It is sacred. It is holy. It is beyond comment or evaluation.

The Highest Truth

You come to oneness not through conformity, but through authenticity. When you have the courage to be yourself, you find the highest truth you are capable of receiving. Finding the highest truth in yourself, you recognize that truth when you see it manifest in others.

Not Prescribing for Others

The man or woman of Spirit trusts others to find their own way. S/he seeks no students or disciples.

Those who seek followers must house and feed them. They will not find freedom, for they do not give it.

Freedom comes when you reject all forms of external authority and when you refuse to be an authority for anyone else. Paradoxically, that is also the moment in which the self becomes Self.

Share your experience? Yes, to be sure! Your story can be of immense help to others. But the boundaries of such an offering are clear. It is YOUR experience you are offering, a story, not a prescription for others. Whatever truth someone else sees in it is the truth he is meant to receive. And this, of course, will be different for each person who hears your story.

Ultimately, you alone are responsible for the beliefs you accept. Someone can tell you terrible lies, but it will never be his responsibility that you believed. So do not waste your time blaming the guru, the cult or the church. Thank them instead. Whether they realized it or not, they have done you a great service. They have taught you clearly what you are to avoid.

Everybody at one time or another gives his power away, only to learn to take it back. That is an important and profound lesson on the spiritual path. Be grateful if you have learned this lesson. It means you are closer to your own truth, and if you are closer to your own truth, you are closer to God, the universal truth.

The True Authority of Your Heart

The true authority of your heart does not submit to the wants and needs of other people, however cleverly disguised. Nor does it submit to your own wants and needs, which are inevitably perceived in fear. The true authority of your heart blesses you in your wholeness. It does not want. It does not need. It does not seek approval from others.

True authority is rock-solid and self-nurtured. It moves perpetually toward its greatest joy without harming others. It knows without hesitation that its joy is not at odds with the joy of others. It serves others not out of sacrifice but through the extension of an inner joy that is constantly bubbling up and spilling over.

The true authority of your heart does not need to gain the approval of others, nor does it desire to please self at the expense of others. It is not drawn outward into other people's dramas, nor inward into the attempt to satisfy personal wants and needs.

Call it God. Call it your higher self. Call it your Christ Mind or your Buddha Nature. Names do not matter. You access this Authority through your stillness, your quiet acceptance of yourself and others, your profound willingness to be present. You sink through the superficial dichotomies of mind into the depths of the heart. And there, not surprisingly, you meet God not as Other, but as Self. In the silence, there is just a single heartbeat. It cannot belong to anyone else, for there is no one else there.

Dying into the Divine

The human must die so that the divine can be born. Not because it is bad. But because it is the shell that holds the spirit, the cocoon that holds the wings of the butterfly.

However, you do not have to wait until the moment

of your physical death for the human to die. The human can die into the divine right now if you are willing to stop playing the victim, if you are willing to stop resisting, defending, hiding, projecting shame and blame.

You cannot fly until you are willing to claim your wings. But once you do, you cannot remain in the dark shadows of your fear.

It is your choice. How would you choose? What would you be: victim or angel?

There is nothing in between! That which appears to exist in between is just the human shell: the being who has not yet chosen, the caterpillar dreaming of wings.

The Light Bearer

You, my friend, are the Christ, the Messiah, the one who brings salvation. You are the one who brings the love you have sought from others, the one who brings release from self-violation and abusive relationships. You are the only one who can step into your experience, own it fully, and lift it up.

Only when you know that you are the light bearer does the darkness disappear. But before you can become the light bearer you must walk through your own darkness. The bearer of the light does not deny the darkness. He walks through it.

When there is nothing about yourself or anyone else that you are afraid to look at, the darkness has no more hold over you. Then you can walk through the darkness and be the light.

To pretend to be the light bearer before you have faced your own fear is to be a pretender, an unhealed healer, a sham. All unhealed healers eventually come off their imaginary pedestals. Where there is only the pretension to light, the darkness still prevails.

To be the light you must embrace the darkness. Your darkness. Everyone's darkness. You must come to terms with the ego mind and see its absolute futility. You must learn to look at fear with love in your heart: your fear, your sister's fear, the fear of the rapist or murderer.

You must know that all fear is alike and all fear is simply a lack of love. Love is the answer to your deepest sense of separation. Not someone else's love. Your love.

Once you take the torch of truth and bring love to the wounded parts of your mind, you take back your power. You surrender your victimhood. You can no longer be unfairly treated because you are the very source of love, acceptance, and forgiveness.

Where does love come from? It comes from you. You are the way, the truth, and the life, just as I was. Don't look for the divine outside yourself. In your blessing of yourself, the entire world is forgiven.

When does the kingdom of Heaven come to Earth? As soon as you are willing to open your heart and walk through your fears.

When does the Messiah come? No, not later, but now. Now is the end of separation, the end of projection, the final death knell of fear. Now.

Do not place salvation in the future or it will never come. Ask for it now. Accept it now. God's kingdom manifests in this moment only.

When does Heaven come? When this moment is enough. When this place is enough. When this friend is enough. When these events and circumstances are acceptable. When you no longer crave something other than what stands before you.

Miracles & Spiritual
Practices

Miracles Cannot be Planned

Miracles do not come from linear, sequential thinking. They cannot be planned. You cannot learn to perform them or to receive them.

Miracles come spontaneously to the heart that has opened and the mind that has surrendered its need to control or to know.

❁

God doesn't ask you to chop off your intellect and believe on faith. S/He makes a far more simple request: "Just stop judging, stop finding fault, stop trying to make life conform to your pictures of reality."

When you experience your life free of the limitations you would place upon it, problems resolve. Relationships move on course. You stop interfering with God's plan.

What is God's plan? It is healing, reconciliation, joyful self-expression and intimate communion. God's agenda is to allow the miraculous to happen at all times. Wherever your ego sees a problem or a limit, God sees an opportunity to love more deeply.

God says: *let go of the past and make room for something new and more wonderful*. You are afraid to do that because you want what is familiar. You want continuity.

If something is continuous, it is not miraculous. Miraculous events are not continuous with what happened before them. They represent a shift of energy, a movement out of past perception. They are unpredictable and unexpected.

You call them miracles because God's hand is in them. But without your permission, they could not take place. Without your surrender of the past, miracles could not come into your lives. You prepare the ground for them. You create the space in which the miraculous occurs.

A Higher Order

All events cohere in a higher order, the meaning of which dawns on those who open their hearts and minds to their experience. No event, no matter how unfortunate, is devoid of purpose.

You are no less holy as a cripple than you are as the person whose broken limbs are mysteriously healed.

Don't be foolish enough to believe that you are bad or unholy if you don't get the miracle you want.

Such thinking comes from looking only at the surface of life. And, if you want to understand the miraculous nature of life, you must look beneath the surface.

Miracles challenge your world view. They urge you to let go of your interpretation of life so that you can see the possibilities that lie beyond it.

Visualization can be powerful. It can alter perception and assist in healing. But I wouldn't suggest that you tie yourself to the train tracks and visualize the train disappearing as it approaches you at sixty miles per hour.

Miracle-mindedness is not demonstrated through the attempt to manipulate physical reality. That is an activity of the ego. The attempt to produce miracles on demand is the activity of a clown, not a spiritual man or woman.

You demonstrate your miracle-mindedness by surrendering to your experience and connecting with God's will for you in each moment. Your job is not to try to alter physical laws, but to work with them.

The Door

I have told you that you will demonstrate miracles in your life just as I did in mine. When you are a loving presence, people will come home to the true Self through you.

You see, it does not matter who the door is. It could be me. It could be you. It could be another brother or sister. The door does not need to be celebrated.

When the door needs to be celebrated, it ceases to be a door. When people grasp the finger pointing to the moon, they can no longer tell where it is pointing.

I never said that you should walk through brick walls or even that you should walk on water. I merely pointed to the open door and asked you if you were ready to enter. And that is all that you need to ask your brother and sister.

One who loves without conditions is never attached to the outcome. People come and go and you never know the whys and wherefores. You think that some people will easily pass through the gate, yet they turn suddenly away. You are convinced that others will never come within sight of the gate, yet they cross the threshold with unexpected grace.

Do not be concerned. It is none of your business who comes and who goes. The covenant is made in every heart and only God knows who is ready and who is not.

My life is the fruit of my practice. So is yours.

What good are lovely sermons if the one who gives them does not practice what s/he preaches? Actions always speak louder than words. People emulate what you do, not what you say.

The Bottomless Well

Your heart is the place where love is born. It is the bottomless well from which you can draw as often as you need to. Every time you come to the well, you drink the waters of life. Your spiritual thirst is quenched. Your sins are forgiven. You are baptized, healed and renewed.

Whenever life feels difficult, there is only one place

that offers you sanctuary. You must learn to make your pilgrimage there on a regular basis.

Don't look outside of yourself for answers. Don't seek refuge in the ideas, opinions and advice of other people. Don't go into your head and try to figure things out. Surrender all of that, and seek the place where love begins, in your own heart. It is your responsibility to reconnect with the Source of love when you need to. No one else can do it for you.

When the spark in your heart is attended to, it grows into a steady flame. When the flame is fed by acts of loving kindness to self and others, it becomes a blazing fire, a source of warmth and light for all who encounter it.

Rituals of Remembering

I do not ask you to meditate or pray for an hour a day, although there is nothing wrong with this. I simply ask you to remember your Divine Essence for five minutes out of each hour, or for one thought out of every ten. Nine thoughts may be about needing to fix yourself or someone else, but let the tenth thought be about that which does not need fixing. Let the tenth thought be about something which is totally acceptable, totally lovable.

This is the rhythm the Sabbath was meant to establish. For six days you could be absorbed in the drama of work and struggle, but on the seventh day you were to remember God. The seventh day was to be a day of rest, of turning inward.

Let the wisdom of the Sabbath be brought into your daily life. Then, when you eat, God will sit at your table. When you speak with your brother, you will remember to say something encouraging to him.

The Sabbath is a ritual of remembering. When you realize this, you can discard the outer shell and find a form of the ritual that helps you remember.

The Silence of the Heart

All the answers that you need can be found in the silence of your heart. You don't have to look to others for solutions or advice. When people come to you saying "I have the answer," send them politely away. Their answer is just as toxic for you as your own judgment of the situation.

Admit "I do not know what this means." And trust the same intelligent force which brought this situation into your life to reveal its significance when it is time.

You don't need to practice elaborate systems of meditation or yoga. Simply cease judging, interpreting, conceptualizing, speculating. Let all that is not "being" fall away and "being" will flower of itself.

This is the most profound practice I can give you. In this simple practice, all the barriers to truth will come down.

A Helpful Practice

Any place and any time in the course of your daily life, you can be doing spiritual practice. Whenever you find yourself getting confused, anxious, fearful, angry, etc., ask yourself "Am I loving myself right now?" This question helps you understand that beneath all fearful thoughts and behaviors lies the refusal to be gentle and loving toward yourself.

Even if your anger or upset feelings are directed toward someone else, you aren't being loving toward yourself. Indeed, the only way that you can be angry at anyone else is to forget to love yourself.

The question "Am I loving myself right now?" reminds you of your only responsibility while here in this embodiment: to love and take care of yourself. When love is established in your heart, it flows automatically to others.

This is anything but a selfish practice. It is a practice that takes you back to your heart, where love originates.

When you are Not Ready to Bless

Another practice that will help you stay centered is to refrain from speaking or acting when you are not ready to bless others. By refusing to make others guilty, you interrupt the cycle of blame and shame. You don't engage their pain with your pain, their anger with your anger, or their unworthiness with your own.

Because you speak and act only when you are able to bless, you stand free of the painful drama of mutual trespass and betrayal. You take care of yourself and others at the deepest level of being. Waves of illusion wash over you, but you stand simply and firmly in the truth that you are.

Illusions

Illusions are born when you stop loving another person or yourself. The only way to dissolve illusions is to start loving right now in this moment.

The Myth of Evil

The New Covenant

The New Covenant asks you to recognize the Kingdom of God in your own heart. That is another way of saying that you reject the idea that God is separate from you. You reject the idea that you are unlovable or that your brother or sister is unlovable. You reject the idea of evil as an idea created in fear. You reject the idea that God's power can be abused.

Accepting your creative power is impossible without your reconciliation with God. For all power comes from Her. You share in that power as an equal partner, but you can never exercise that power apart from Her.

The power of God's love cannot be abused. It can be rejected, denied, hidden. But all rejection, denial, and secret guilt have limits. Truth can be distorted but it can never be completely eradicated or denied. A tiny light always remains in the deepest darkness. And that light will always be found when the desire to find it arises.

Everything is God

Everything is God, including that which tries to live without God. For what tries to live without God is simply a part of God that doesn't accept Itself. It is God pretending not to be God.

People who do "evil" acts are not separate from God even though they feel separate. They feel unloved and act in unloving ways. But God has not stopped loving them. God is not able to stop loving anyone. For God is love, always love, in every moment.

Every sin is but a temporary moment of separation. It cannot be final. Every child who strays from God's love will return, because it is too painful to be separate from the Source of love. When the pain becomes too great, every wounded child turns back. There are no exceptions.

40 Days in the Desert

When I was in the desert for forty days, I experienced every voice of fear you can imagine. These were not devils outside of me that had come to tempt me. They were voices in my own mind that caused me to doubt myself or others.

You too have your time in the desert when you must face your own doubts and fears. This time of inner testing usually precedes your acceptance of your purpose here. For if you cannot move through your own fears, how can you begin to deal with the fears of others when they project them onto you?

If you are not whole and strong in yourself, how can you be a beacon of love and light for others? The kind of strength and integration I am talking about here is not to be taken lightly. Can you meet your devils and learn to love them? Can you love when fear comes up?

Before you begin your life work, these questions must be answered. You must enter the darkness of your own psyche carrying the light of awareness. Every fear which undermines your self-esteem must be faced.

Peace will not come to the world until it comes into your heart. And it cannot come into your heart as long as you see enemies or "evil" people outside of you. Every evil you perceive in the world points to an unforgiving place in your heart that is calling out for healing.

⁂

Apart from your judgments there is no hell. Yet you pretend there is a "devil" apart from your beliefs, or an "evil" not connected to your judgments. It is not true. Every evil comes from your judgments and every devil comes from the projection of your shame.

Do not see the drama happening outside of you or you will lose the key to the kingdom. Those who see themselves as victims will not be empowered. Those who see themselves as weak will not overcome the obstacles in their lives.

The drama of shame and blame is happening only in your mind and that is where it must be dealt with. Believe for a moment "I am lovable; I am acceptable; I am worthy;" and your victimhood comes to an end. Believe "I am capable of loving my brother regardless of how he acts toward me" and the invisible bonds of projection fall away.

You are the one who holds the key to the kingdom. If you offer committed love, love that overlooks faults and soars above judgments, how can any less be returned to you?

This is a circular world. What goes out comes back in and vice versa. It only appears to be linear. It only appears to exist in time and space.

If you keep looking for the devil in others, you will not find him. The devil is your own angelic presence defiled. It is all of your forgetting, all of your self-violation. It is the wounded one, the crucified one, the angel who has fallen from the sky into the muck, into the savage pull of worldly incarnation.

The AntiChrist

The AntiChrist is the personification of the collective ego. He seeks salvation and peace by controlling others. His attempt to force reconciliation never works, because what lives by the sword dies by the sword. Wrong means always lead to wrong ends.

However, even the Antichrist is not evil. He is simply starved for love. Being starved for love, he tries to buy it, demand it, control it. By so doing, he pushes love further away. The more love eludes him, the more vicious he gets. His fear begets the fear of others.

This recalcitrant being lives inside of each one of you. He is simply the ego mind: the scared, unhappy, angry little kid inside of you who feels unfairly treated and constantly manipulates others in his search for love.

He is formidable only because you judge him and resist him. Don't push him away anymore. Take this abused child in your arms and rock him. Hold him; speak gently to him. Love him as your own precious child.

When you have embraced the wounded child within, his angelic presence is revealed. Lucifer (his name means light bearer) is, after all, a fallen angel. In your love, his fall is broken and he finds his wings. In his redemption, yours is guaranteed.

God does not come from on high to free you from a world of your own making. Why would He take you from what you have chosen?

God comes through your gesture of acceptance toward your ego mind with all its fearful imaginings. He comes in the love and compassion you bring to the wounded one within you and outside of you. He comes when you reach down to embrace the dark wings that hover in front of the door of your fear.

These wings will not hurt you. They will not rob you of your innocence, no matter how much abuse has been given or received. See through the dark disguise and come into the warmth of these wings. There is a door here that leads straight to the heart.

You cannot come to God if you don't go through the dark night of the soul. All your fear and shame must be raised. All your feelings of separation must come up for healing. How can you rise from the ashes of your pain unless you will acknowledge the pain?

If you pretend the wound isn't there, you can't begin your spiritual journey. Don't deny that it hurts. Come into your pain. It is not what you think it is.

When you have the courage to approach the wall of your fear, it turns into a doorway. Come through this door. I am waiting for you on the other side.

The Dreamer Awakens

You are the dreamer of the darkness and the one who brings the light. You are tempter and savior rolled in one. This you will come to know if you do not know it already.

The Reign of Christ

Christ does not blame others. He does not fight back. He does not resist evil.

The strongest power in the universe seems to be so easily overpowered, crucified and forgotten. But it is not so. All who attack the Christ must return to serve Him.

That is the karmic law. Your relationship with every other person is ultimately a reflection of an attitude you have toward yourself.

Healing Our Wounds

Pain Brings Awareness

Pain is a messenger. It brings awareness. It tells you where and how you have betrayed yourself. That is important. Until you are aware of the self-violation, your journey to healing cannot begin.

Pain is not a punishment. It is a call to become conscious, to raise your hidden suffering into awareness,

It isn't easy to acknowledge your pain and the cry for love behind it. But this is how you heal. You become aware of the dark, disenfranchised aspects of self and bring them into conscious awareness. You redeem them. You bring your darkness to the light.

Most of you project what you dislike or are afraid of in yourself onto others. If you are afraid of your power, you project it onto some powerful, charismatic figure through whom you try to live. When that person takes advantage of you or betrays you, you forget that it was you who gave your power away to this person.

Reclaiming all of yourself means facing the parts of

yourself of which you are afraid or ashamed. Other people who embody these qualities merely help you discover them in yourself. That is why relationship is such an important tool in the work of inner integration.

Blaming others prevents you from healing. If you want to heal, take responsibility for your behavior and see the pattern of abuse you are engaged in. Understand how self-depreciation invites trespass and learn to value and appreciate yourself.

Remember, every abusive relationship offers you the opportunity to say no to what does not honor you. Saying no to another person, of course, implies an awareness that you have tended to say "yes" in the past.

You establish the conditions for abuse by accepting conditional love. You say yes to self-degradation in exchange for the security and approval you want. You say yes to fear by bargaining for love.

Now you know it will not work. Love cannot be bargained for.

When love is given to you without conditions you

know it. It doesn't ask from you more than you can give. It doesn't manipulate or demand. It accepts you as you are and blesses you.

If you do not know how to create this blessing for yourself, how can you receive it from another? Practice it. Practice accepting yourself just as you are. Then you will know what love is and you will recognize it when it comes into your life.

If you love yourself conditionally, you will draw others into your life who do the same. You cannot receive from others what you are unable or unwilling to give to yourself.

When you know what you want, please ask for it. When someone says "I'm sorry. I can't offer you that," tell them "No problem. It will come in good time." Stay focused on what you want, regardless of what people offer you. Reject all the conditions with which love and attention are offered to you. Hold fast to the truth of your heart, accepting no less than you have promised to yourself.

And, in time, it comes, because you have been faithful to yourself. Because you have answered the call within your own heart, the Beloved appears unannounced at your doorstep. This is not a magical formula, but the fruit of a committed spiritual practice.

In the eyes of Spirit, people are completely equal. The rich man has no more happiness than the poor man. In his heart, he has the same struggle, the same hurt. The wealthy doctor who has lost a son to AIDS has the same pain that the woman on welfare has when she loses her daughter.

Pain is the great equalizer. It brings you to your knees. It makes you more humble and sensitive to the needs of others. It undermines all hierarchies.

If you have touched your own pain deeply, you know this. You feel compassion when you see others in pain. You do not need to push them away, nor do you need to try to fix them. You just hold them deeply in your heart. You offer them a hug and some words of encouragement. You know what they are going through.

The world builds people up and it takes people down.

There is no permanence in the world. Fame and ignominy, poverty and riches, happiness and despair run hand in hand. You can't experience one side without experiencing the other.

If you haven't touched your own pain, you are just postponing the inevitable. It is only a matter of time before you have to acknowledge to yourself, if not to others, your dirty laundry: your judgments, your fears, your neediness, your suicidal thoughts.

For many people, it is easier to let others see the pasteboard mask than the contorted face behind it. They are proud of the spiritual adult, but ashamed of the wounded child.

However, those who have the courage to face their pain pull the mask away. They give themselves permission to be authentic and to grow. Their willingness to be emotionally present with what they are feeling opens a sacred passageway. Closed hearts start to pulsate, bodies begin to breathe, and blocked energies are released. This is the first step in the healing process.

Other steps follow, for healing means movement. It doesn't mean falling in love with pain, holding onto it, or building an identity around it. It is not a stationary train, but a moving one. Once you get on it, it takes you where you need to go.

Pain is the great equalizer. It enables you to be honest and authentic. It empowers you to ask for unconditional love and support from others and to be willing to offer the same in return. It connects you with a healing community of human beings whose shells of denial are cracking.

The attachment to pain is just as dysfunctional as the denial of it. Yet some people see that their pain gets them lots of attention. They build a whole identity around being a victim.

However, the authentic person is not a professional story teller. He is not a confession artist. He does not need to be the center of attention to feel good about himself.

The authentic person tells his story because the telling of it is an act of healing. As he tells it, he comes to a more profound understanding and acceptance of what happened. As he heals, others heal with him.

The moment he has integrated his experience, he no longer needs to tell his story. If he insists on telling it, it becomes a crutch that he leans on, even though his limbs have healed. He becomes more entertainer than witness, and his story—more polished than heart-felt—no longer empowers people.

The acceptance of pain brings a shift away from disease toward increased ease. It allows you to take the next step on your journey. When you share authentically, you empower yourself and others. You move on. They move on. A life of pain is no longer called for.

While pain and suffering are universal phenomena, they are temporary ones. They touch every life at one time or another. But they are not constant companions. They are messengers.

To say that the messenger is not present when he is standing at your door is utter foolishness. You need to answer the door and hear what he has to say. But when the message has been heard, the messenger can leave. His job is over.

When suffering becomes a status symbol, a culture of unhealed healers is born. When it becomes "chic" to be a victim of childhood trauma or sexual abuse, therapists too easily get away with putting words in their clients' mouths. Memories of events that never happened are enshrined on the altar. Incidents of minor insensitivity or carelessness are exaggerated and painted with the language of guilt. Everyone imagines that the worst must have happened. This is hysteria, not healing. It is a new form of abuse.

Instead of inquiring into what happened and allowing the inner wounded one to speak, a professional label is placed on the wound. Instead of empowering the victim to find his voice and connect with his experience, his voice is squelched once again. He is given someone else's opinion of what happened to him and, in order to gain approval, he tells the story the authority figure asks him to tell.

The therapist projects her own unhealed wounds onto her client. Her subjectivity is taken for objectivity by the courts. Families are separated. More children are punished. The chain of abuse continues.

The attachment to pain is debilitating. The embellishment, exaggeration or fabrication of pain is insane.

Just as the creation of a priestly class of authority figures undermined the organic spirituality of the church, so the creation of a new class of therapist/healer author-ity figures undermines the ability of individuals to access the healing that is their birthright.

You can't make anyone heal any more than you can make people act in a moral way. Healing is a voluntary act. It happens as people are ready. Many people in ther-apy have no intention to heal. Many people dispensing therapeutic advice have no commitment to their own healing. For these people, therapists and clients alike, therapy is a form of denial.

Letting the wound heal by itself is just as important as ministering to the wound. You forget that the spiritual essence of the person does the healing, not the therapist or healer.

The compulsion to heal is just as vicious as the com-pulsion to wound. Indeed, they are different faces of the same coin.

The true healer respects the inner healing ability of her client. She helps her client make the connections that are ready to be made. She advocates integration, gentleness, patience. Thus, her clients get stronger. They heal and move on.

If you are working as a therapist, encourage your

clients to avoid the extremes of denying their pain or embellishing it. Pain must be faced, not imagined. If it is there, it will express itself authentically. It will speak with its own voice. Your job is to invite the voice to speak, not to give it the words to say.

Finding out what happened to you is the first step in the process of healing trauma. Secrets need to be disclosed or discovered.

Don't deny what happened. Don't make it up. Just acknowledge what happened and be with it. That is what starts the shift from untruth to truth, from secrets to revelation, from hidden discomfort to the conscious awareness of pain.

Pain is a door you walk through when you are ready. Until then, you are the doorkeeper, the sentinel who stands guard and decides whom to exclude and whom to let in.

It is okay not to be ready. It's okay to exclude people or situations that feel unsafe. You are in charge of your own healing process. You decide how fast to go. Don't let anyone else – including your therapist—dictate the pace of your healing process. It must be self-directed.

Others will always have ideas, suggestions, plans for you. Thank them for their concern, but be clear that you, not they, are making the decisions in your life.

Don't accept anyone else's authority over you and don't accept authority over anyone else. Claim your freedom and offer freedom to others.

Do not seek approval from others or offer it when others seek it from you. Get out of the approval business.

There is only one person here who needs to give and receive love and that is you. Give love to yourself and include others in that love. If they do not wish to be included, let them go. You do not need another detour, another useless journey.

Be steadfast in your love for yourself. Let that be your number one commitment. Then, you will attract others into your life who are happy to be themselves. They will not come to you making demands or trying to take control of your life.

When someone makes you an offer you think you can't refuse, learn to refuse it. Don't betray yourself, regardless of the price.

The tempter will always come to you offering extraordinary gifts. Don't be fooled. He seems to have supernatural powers, but they are not real. He is just your brother moving off course, trying to draw you into his drama of self-abuse.

Don't say yes to abuse. Remember, you are already whole. You lack nothing. Relax and breathe. This too will pass.

But the tempter shouts out: "No. You are not okay. You are lonely. You need companionship. You need a better job. You need a better relationship. You need more money, more sex, more notoriety; all of this will I give to you."

Surely, you have heard this pitch before! Some knight in shining armor or damsel in distress always appears when you are feeling low. Where has it gotten you in the past? How many knights or damsels have sped off on their steeds leaving a trail of blood and tears?

Yet this one seems better than the last. S/he is more sincere, more sensitive, more grounded, more _____. You fill in the blank. It is your drama, not mine.

If you look deeply enough, you will see that every pitch is the same. Every invitation to self-betrayal has the same sugar coated promises and the same heart-wrenching core.

Those who seek salvation in another lose touch with self. They go off like Quixote on the great horizontal journey. And they always find damsels to rescue and windmills to fight.

But, in the end, they return home tired, wounded, and lacking in faith. The horizontal journey defeats everyone who takes it. There is no salvation to be found in the world.

Salvation is found at home, in your own heart. It is there that you learn to love the disowned, rejected parts of yourself. It is there that you discover your wholeness and become rooted in the blessing of God's abundance and grace.

The Self is unassailable. You cannot put holes in it. You can only pretend to hurt or be hurt. You cannot be separated from the Source of love, because you are love incarnate. You are the shining one dreaming the dream of abuse. You are the angel walking as wounded.

Pretending to be an angel when you feel like an abused kid does not contribute to your awakening. But neither does holding onto the wound.

When the wound is addressed with love, it heals. The healing can be instantaneous or it can take a lifetime, but victimization does stop and healing does happen. The drama of suffering does comes to an end.

Awakening is not a wrenching process, but a gentle giving up of blame and shame. It is not that love makes "evil" go away, but that all perceptions of "evil" fade away in the presence of love. In the end, it is as if the wound never happened. At best, you could say it was a dream of abuse, a dream from which you have gloriously awakened.

Love Without Conditions

Conditional Love

You have learned conditional love from people whose love for you was compromised by their own guilt and fear. These have been your role models. You need not be ashamed of this. You need only be aware of it as a fact.

From the time you were an infant, you were conditioned to value yourself only when people responded positively to you. You learned that your self worth was established externally. That was the fundamental error, which has perpetuated itself throughout your life. Your parents' experience was no different from yours.

In the process of healing, you learn to value yourself as you are, here and now, without conditions. Thus, you are "born again," or "re-parented," not by other authority figures, but by the Source of Love inside yourself.

No one else can do this for you. People can assist and encourage, but no one can teach you how to love yourself. That is the work of each individual soul.

The experience of unconditional love begins in your heart, not in someone else's. Don't make your ability to love yourself conditional on someone else's ability to love you. Your attempt to find love outside yourself always fails, because you cannot receive from another something you haven't given to yourself.

For most of your life, you have accepted other people's ideas and opinions as the truth about you. Yet what mother, dad, teacher, or minister said about you is just their opinion. Unfortunately, you internalize the feedback you get from others and you develop your self-image based on it. In other words, your opinion of yourself is not based on what you know and find out about you, but on what other people tell you.

Where then is the "real you" in the equation of self and other? The real you is the unknown factor, the essence that has been heavily clothed in the judgments and interpretations you have accepted about yourself and your experience.

This is true for everyone, not just for you. People relate to one another not as authentic, self-realized beings, but as personae, masks, roles, identities. Often, people have more than one mask that they wear, depending on whom they are with and what is expected of them.

The true Self gets lost and forgotten among all these disguises. And its great gift of authenticity is not consciously acknowledged.

Self Vs. Persona

The true Self is not bound by the limitations, judgments and interpretations with which the persona lives. Indeed, it can be said that Self and persona live in different worlds. The world of Self is bright and self-fulfilling. The world of persona is dark and self-defeating. While Self finds light within and radiates it toward others, persona finds only darkness within and seeks the light from others.

Self says "I am." Persona says "I am this" or "I am that." Self lives and expresses unconditionally. Persona lives and expresses conditionally. Self is motivated by love and says "I can." Persona lives in fear and says "I can't." Persona complains, apologizes and makes excuses. Self accepts, integrates and gives its gift.

You are Self, but believe yourself to be your persona.

As long as you operate as persona, you will have experiences that confirm your beliefs about yourself and others. When you realize that all personae are just masks you and others have agreed to wear, you will learn to see behind the masks.

When that happens, you will glimpse the radiance of the Self within and without. You will see a bright being, eminently worthy and capable of love, dynamically creative, generous and self-fulfilling. That is your inmost nature. And that is the nature of all beings in your experience.

When you accept who you really are, your arguments with others cease. For you no longer do battle with their personae. You see the light behind the mask. Your light and their light are all that matter.

When you contact the truth about you, you recognize that a great deal that you have come to accept about you is false. You are not better or worse than others. You are not stupid, or brilliant, or handsome, or ugly. Those are just judgments someone made that you accepted. None of them is true.

When you know the truth about you, you know that you are not your body, although you need to accept it and take care of it. You are not your thoughts and feelings, although you need to be aware of them and see how they are creating the drama of your life. You are not the roles that you are playing - husband or wife, mother or father, son or daughter, employee or boss, secretary or plumber - although you need to make peace with whatever role you choose to play. You are not anything external. You are not anything that can be defined by something or someone else.

The purpose of your journey here is to discover the Self and leave the persona behind. You are here to find out that the Source of love lies within your own consciousness.

You do not have to seek love outside of yourself. Indeed, the very act of seeking it in the world will prevent you from recognizing it within yourself.

You can't see the light in others until you see it in yourself. Once you see it in yourself, there is no one in whom you do not see the light. It does not matter if they see it or not. You know it's there. And it is the light you address when you speak to them.

The world of personae is a chaotic and reactive world. It is fueled by fear and judgment. It is real only because you and others believe in it and define yourselves by the conditions you find there. But those conditions are not ultimate reality. They are simply a collective drama of your making. Yes, the drama has its own rules, its costumes, its inter-relationships and its plan of action. But none of this matters when you take your costume off and step off the stage.

Mind you, the play will go on. It does not depend on you alone. But when you know it's just a play, you can choose to participate in it or not. If you participate, you will do so remembering who you are, understanding the part that you play without being attached to it.

Suffering ends when your attachment to all conditions dissolves. Then, you rest in the Self, the embodiment of love, the Source of creation itself.

Solitude

Solitude is necessary for your emotional health, whether you are living alone or living with another. Solitude gives you the time and space to integrate your experience.

Having lots of experiences means nothing if you do not take the time to learn from them. Jumping from activity to activity or relationship to relationship wreaks havoc on your emotional core. The time you take to integrate your experience is as important as the time you take to have the experience itself.

Every breath you take has three movements: an inhalation, a pause, and an exhalation. The inhalation is for the taking in of experience. The pause is for its assimilation. And the exhalation is for the release of experience. While the pause is just a second or two, it is essential for the integrity of the breath.

Solitude allows you to pause. The quality of your life depends upon it. Your energy and enthusiasm arise from it.

If you drop out this part, your life will be an empty shell. A great deal may pass in and out of it. But nothing will stick. There will be no assimilation of experience or growth in consciousness.

The Fountainhead

The reason that you are looking for love from other people is that you do not realize that love comes only from your own consciousness. It has nothing to do with anyone else. Love comes from your willingness to think loving thoughts, experience loving feelings, and act in trusting, love-inspired ways. If you are willing to do this, your cup will run over. You will constantly have the love that you need, and you will take delight in offering it to others.

The fountainhead of love is within your own heart. Don't look to others to provide the love you need. Don't blame others for withholding their love from you. You don't need their love. You need your love. Love is the only gift you can give yourself. Give it to yourself and the universe resounds with a big "Yes!" Withhold it and the game of hide and seek continues: "looking for love in all the wrong places."

There is only one place you can look for love and find it. No one who has ever looked there has been disappointed.

As long as you deny the Self by seeking it through another, you will have trespass and abuse.

If you want love, bring love to the places in yourself that feel unloved. If you want light, bring it to the dark places of your mind. Bring it to the fear and the shame, to the sadness, to the perceived lack of purpose or hope.

That light is within you. It is not separate from the darkness. It is a quality of the darkness itself. When you get to absolute pitch blackness, there illumination is found. Blackest black becomes radiant. Sadness turns to unaccountable joy. Despair turns to hope without measure.

In one pole, you find the other.

The only way out of the detour of co-dependent relationships is to befriend and honor the Self. Then one can build relationship on the truth of self-coherence. This is the new paradigm of relationship.

In the old relationship paradigm, the commitment to self is vitiated by the commitment to other. In seeking to please the other, self is abandoned. Since the abandoned self is incapable of love, this constitutes a vicious cycle of attraction and rejection. First the self is excluded, and then the other is excluded.

All genuine relationship must be built on the foundation of one's acceptance of and love for self. That is the primary spiritual gesture, the one that opens the door to the potential for intimacy.

True & False Prophets

Love Takes No Hostages

One who loves without conditions places no limits on his freedom nor on anyone else's. He does not try to keep love, for to try to keep it is to lose it.

Love is a gift that must constantly be given as it is asked for in each moment. It takes no hostages, makes no bargains, and cannot be compromised by fear.

Not Fixing Others

If you want to be kind to others, you need to accept them the way they are and stop trying to judge, analyze, interpret, or change their lives. When you try to fix others or give them advice, you are trespassing against them.

When you trust others to find their own answers, you treat them as spiritual equals. You offer them respect and freedom. You trust the truth within them to light their way. That is love in action. That is the kind of unconditional love I ask you to offer one another.

Don't make rules for other people. That will just take the focus away from your life. Let others find their own way. Support them. Encourage them. Cheer them on. But don't think you know what's good for them. You don't know. Nor will you ever know.

Stay in your life. Stay in your heart. Everything that you need to fulfill your destiny will be found within. Listen to your guidance, honor it, act on it, be committed to it, and it will unfold. When you are joined with your own divine nature, the doors you need to walk through will open to you.

Nobody comes into embodiment with an empty plate. Everyone has at least a scrap or two to digest. (Some have seven course meals! But I'm not going to point any fingers!)

Your responsibility is to deal with what's on your plate as happily as you can. Don't interfere in the lives of others or you will have a second or a third helping to dispose of.

Stay detached from what someone else does or does not do. Don't even have an opinion about it. Just let it be.

Don't borrow someone else's experience. Don't try to give someone else your experience.

Sleep in your own bed. Prepare your own food. Clean up after yourself. Practice taking care of yourself and let others do the same for themselves.

That is your job. You are not here to do for others what they must do for themselves.

It is a revelation to some of you to know that you are not here to rescue others from their pain, but merely to walk through your own. No one else can do that for you. It is your essential responsibility and will be throughout this embodiment. Even when you join your life with another person's life, this responsibility stays with you. Whenever you lose sight of it, or try to give it to someone else, you inevitably pay the price.

If each of you would nurture the truth within your hearts, you would collectively give birth to a very different world. It would be a world of realization, not sacrifice, a world of equality, not prejudice, a world of insight and respect, not collusion and despair.

Teachers Who Empower

Authentic spiritual teachers claim no authority over others. They do not pretend to have the answers for others.

They do not preach. They do not try to fix. They simply accept people as they are and encourage them to find their own truth.

They don't deny the darkness, but they don't oppose it either. They just gently encourage the light. They know the light itself will heal all wounds.

Authentic teachers don't believe that people are evil or that the world is doomed. They understand the universal cry for acceptance and love. And that is what they give.

Do they give food and medical supplies if they are needed? Of course, but they also remember to whom they are giving them. They know that food is helpful, but it is not what is being asked for.

What is asked for is love. Love is the real food. Love is what they give.

If you are wise, you will not follow anyone. Then you will not be misled.

But if you must find a teacher or a leader, look for one who empowers you to hear the truth in your own heart. Look for one who loves you without seeking to control you. Find a teacher who honors you and treats you with dignity and respect.

Anyone who claims a special knowledge and sells it for a price is a false prophet. Anyone who needs you to bow down, agree with his opinions, or carry out his agenda is a false prophet. Anyone who asks for money or sexual favors in return for spiritual guidance is a false prophet. Anyone who encourages you to give away your power, your self-respect or your dignity is a false prophet. Do not abide with such people.

Do not seek the company of one who denies you the

freedom to be yourself. Do not accept a teacher who tries to make decisions for you. Do not let anyone dictate to you or control your life.

On the other hand, do not dictate to others or seek to take away their freedom to decide what they want. Any attempt to do so simply binds you to the wheel of suffering.

What you give to others is what you get back. Do not be a victimizer or a victim. Be yourself and allow others to be themselves.

Love is the only door to a spiritual life. Without love, there are just dogmas and rigid, fearful beliefs. Without love, there is no compassion or charity.

Those who judge others, preach to them, and seek to redeem them are just projecting their own fear and inadequacy. They use the words of religion as a substitute for the love they are unable to give or receive.

Many of those who are most forlorn and cut off from love live in the shadow of the pulpit and mount the steps of judgment every Sunday to spread the message of their own fear. Do not judge them, for they are in their own painful way crying out for love. But do not accept the guilt they would lay at your feet. It is not yours.

Those who live a genuinely spiritual life—regardless of the tradition they follow—are centered in their love for God and their fellow beings. When they meet, they have only good wishes and praises for one another. For them, labels mean nothing.

For those who practice their faith, God is the only King of Kings, and men and women, no matter what they believe, are absolute, unconditional equals. All are equally loved and valued by God. There are no outcasts, no heathens.

I have said it before and I will say it again: Religious dogma, self-righteousness, and false pride create division, ostracism, and alienation. They are the tools of judgment, not of love.

Those who find fault with others are not following my teaching. My disciples learn to look upon all that happens with an open heart and an open mind. They grow increasingly willing to surrender their narrow beliefs and prejudices. Their life is their teaching, and it is lived with loving deeds, not with harsh, unforgiving words.

It is better to remain neutral than to speak or act without insight and understanding. Put down your Bibles, your Sutras, your holy books. Don't insist that others live the way you think they should live. If you are concerned about others, love them. Demonstrate that you are capable of speaking and acting in a loving, compassionate way. This will get people's attention much more than preaching will.

Your job is not to preach to others, but to find the truth of your heart. You alone know what course of action is best for the fulfillment of your purpose here. But that knowledge is often buried deeply in the heart. Sometimes, it takes a lot of listening to connect with your own wisdom. In some cases, connecting to yourself is not possible until you stop listening to what other people think you should do.

The path I have laid out for you is an open one. Anyone who wants to can follow it. No prerequisites are necessary: no baptisms, confessions or communions. Nothing external can prevent you from embracing my teaching.

But this does not mean that you will be ready to walk this path. If you are still holding onto dogma or creeds, you will not be able to take the first step. If you are convinced that you or anyone else is evil or guilty, you cannot step forth. If you think you already have the answers, you may begin to walk, but you will be on a different path.

My path is open to all, yet few follow it. Few are willing to give up what they think they know to learn what they know not yet. This is how it was when I first walked the path, and it is how it is today. Many are called, but few answer the call.

Finding the Good

You live in a world where everyone is made guilty. Most teachings come down on you like a sledgehammer, offering correction at best, condemnation at worst.

My teaching is not like that. I tell you that you are not evil. You are not guilty, no matter what you have done, no matter how many mistakes you have made. I recall you to the truth about yourself. Your challenge is to open your heart to that truth.

How do you do this? You do this by refusing to condemn others, by not judging, not complaining, not finding fault. You do this by celebrating your relationships and feeling grateful for the love and nurturing that you have in your life. You focus on what is there, not on what is not there. By finding the good in your life, you reinforce it and extend it to others.

Not Condemning

Only those who are full of pride think that they have exclusive understanding of the truth and the right to judge others. Those who are humble understand that they have no right to judge others.

I am not one to condemn adultery, or divorce, or abortion. For if I were to condemn these situations, those involved in them would be crucified. We would have yet another Inquisition, another holy war pitting good against evil, just against unjust.

My job is not to condemn, but to understand and to bless. My job is to see the fear in people's eyes and remind them that they are loved.

If that is my job, why would I have you beat and burn

and excommunicate those who are most in need of your love? Would you bring me to the level of your fear, put your words in my mouth and attribute them to me? My friend, stop and behold yourself. You have misunderstood. You are mistaken. My teaching is about love, not about judgment, condemnation, or punishment.

Two Rules

I have given you only two rules: to love God and to love one another. Those are the only rules you need. Do not ask me for more. Do not ask me to take sides in your soap opera battles. Am I pro-life or pro-choice? How could I be one without also being the other? It is not possible.

When the truth comes to you, you will no longer need to attack your brother. Even if you think you are right and he is wrong, you will not attack him with "the truth," but offer him your understanding and your support. And together you will move closer to the truth because of the love and gentleness you share.

Every time I give a teaching, someone makes it into a stick to beat people with. Please, my friends, words that are used to beat people up cannot come from me.

I have offered you the key to the door within. Please use it, and do not worry about the thoughts and actions of others. Work on yourself. If you would serve this teaching, learn it first. Do not be a mouthpiece for words and beliefs you have not brought fully into the rhythms of your life.

All who extend my teaching do so from the same level of consciousness as me. Otherwise what they extend cannot be my teaching.

Equality for All

Women have an equal place in my teaching. They have always have had that place and they always will have it. Those who have denied women their rightful place in my church are not following my teaching.

Gays and lesbians, blacks, Asians, Hispanics, born-agains, fundamentalists, Buddhists, Jews, lawyers and politicians all have a place in the community of faith. Everyone is welcome. No one should be excluded. And all who participate in the community should have the opportunity to serve in leadership positions.

My teaching has never been exclusive or hierarchical.

You have imposed your prejudices and your judgments on the truth that I taught. You have taken the house of worship and made it into a prison of fear and guilt. My friends, you are mistaken in your beliefs.

But it is not too late for you to learn from your mistakes. Repent from your unkind actions and make amends to those whom you have injured or judged unfairly. Your mistakes do not condemn you unless you insist on holding onto them. Let them go. You can grow. You can change. You can be wiser than you once were. You can stop being a mouthpiece for fear and become a spokesperson for forgiveness and love.

No ship has ever been refused refuge in the harbor of forgiveness. No matter what you have said or done, I will welcome you home with open arms. All you need to do is to confess your mistakes and be willing to let them go.

If you look carefully, you will notice that those who have the greatest need to tell others what to do have the least faith in themselves. They haven't even begun to hear the voice in their own hearts; yet they are up on a soap-box telling others what to do.

It's not uncommon for people to build a temple over a ditch and call it God's sanctuary. I have told you many times to be careful. Things are not always as they seem. Wolves are disguised in sheep's clothing. Prisons of fear and judgment masquerade as temples of love and forgiveness.

It helps to keep your eyes open. Don't join the crusade until you see the fruits of people's actions. Words are often cheap and misleading.

No One Knows More than You Do

I ask you to remember that no one knows more than you do. No one has anything to give you that you do not already have.

Forget your teachers and gurus, your cults of secular and parochial knowledge. Forget your dogmas, esoterica and metaphysics. None of this will bring you freedom from suffering and pain. It will only add to the burden you carry.

Be realistic about your experience here. There is only one person who needs to wake up and that is you. Those who have a gift to give you will not withhold it. Those who withhold information or love from you, have no gift to give.

Beware of those who would make you jump through hoops or stand in line. They are just lining their pockets at your expense. Do not tolerate the idea that salvation lies somewhere else. It doesn't.

If you allow it, people will be only too glad to prescribe for you or take your freedom away. Don't live by someone else's rules. Live by God's rules.

Hold the self in high regard. It is and must remain unassailable. Hold others in high regard. They must always be honored and set free.

But clearly and with good humor let go of relationships with people who would tell you what to think or what to do. Don't buy the idea that there is something out there to achieve if only you were better behaved, more worthy, more spiritual, more intelligent…you fill in the blank.

Don't line the pockets of those who make empty promises to you. It doesn't matter what they promise: more security, more money, more peace of mind, more enlightenment.

My friend, you are already enlightened. You already

have absolute security. You already have peace of mind and all of the resources you need to fulfill your creative purpose. There is only one thing that you do not have. And that is the awareness that all this is true.

And nobody can give you that awareness. Not me, not some used car salesman, not some swami peddling samadhi. If someone tells you he can, it's time for a belly laugh. Put your arm around him and tell him that's the best joke you've heard in fifty years.

Do you hear me? Nobody can give you that awareness! Awareness is not a gift, but a gesture of the self, an energetic movement to be present and embrace life. Awareness exists a priori in all beings.

Simply desire to be aware and awareness is. It comes and goes with the breath. If you want to be aware, breathe! Breathe in to embrace this moment. Breathe out to release it. Breathe, breathe, breathe. Each breath is an act of awareness.

If I came to your doorstep and told you I was selling breaths for $5 million a piece, you would think that was pretty funny, would you not? You would tell me, "that's very nice, brother, but I already have all the breaths I need." Of course you do.

But you keep forgetting that you have them. You keep buying the insurance policy, falling in love with prince or princess charming, chasing doctor I can make you feel good or swami I've got it all come and get it for five bucks. You know, they all have such long names, it's a wonder you can pronounce them!

Take a breath, my friend. That's right, a deep breath. Nobody has what you need. Did you hear me? Nobody!

You see, you really are all alone here. But it's not as problematic as you think, because there is no part of you that's missing. If you just hang around yourself long enough without giving your power away to others, you will retrieve all the fragmented and dissociated aspects of yourself, for no other reason than they never went away. They just got covered over in your race for the exit.

"Just hang around and you'll get it." Great advice from a holy man, right? "I guess we better send this guy to entrepreneurship training or a spirituality and business workshop or he won't make a living."

I have news for you, friends. I don't need to make a living. I AM a living. And so are you. Just hang around and you'll get it. Because you never lost it. You just pretended to lose it.

One moment you were fully present, and then the next moment your body was there, but your mind was on vacation in the Bahamas. Now, after thirty years or however long it's been, you can bring yourself back, claim your body, and be present in the next moment.

Can you believe that thirty years passed between one breath and another? It may seem strange, but I'm telling you it is a common experience. You needn't be embarrassed.

The next time someone asks how old you are, just tell the truth. "People say I'm forty-five, but I've only taken four breaths!"

I'm just kidding you. Or am I? How many breaths have you taken with complete awareness?

Don't worry about the past. Just begin now. Breathe and claim your life. Breathe and let go of all the mental and emotional crutches you have carried. Breathe and release all the words ever said to you by authority figures.

Breathe and soften. Breathe and strengthen. Breathe and be. You are authentic. You are intact. You are a child of the great Spirit that animates us all.

Standing for the Truth

Renegotiating Commitments

Abuse and betrayal happen when plans are held rigidly or agreements are broken in fear. If you make a commitment and don't feel comfortable keeping it, it is your responsibility to communicate this to the people involved. At all times, you best honor others by telling the truth about your experience.

Ambivalence

To say "yes" or "no" to another person is a clear communication. But to say "no" and mean "yes" or to say "yes" and mean "no" creates the conditions for abuse.

Saying No to the False

Need I remind you that commitment to the truth is not popular? Often it means saying "yes" when others would say "no, or saying "no" when others would say "yes."

Many of you cannot imagine that saying "no" can be a loving act. Yet it is very easy to say "no" in a loving way. If your child is putting his hand on a hot stove, you say "no" quickly and firmly. You do not want him to hurt himself. And then you put your arm around him and reassure him that you love him.

How many times does your brother come to you with his hand on the stove? You cannot support behavior that you know will be hurtful to another person. And you don't want your friends to support that kind of behavior in you.

A friend speaks her truth and then reminds you that you are free to make your own choice. She is willing to share her experience, but she doesn't try to impose her opinion on you.

You can't be a friend if you are not willing to tell the truth. But honesty alone is not enough. Honesty and humility must go hand in hand. Your humility says to your brother "this is the way that I see it. I may be right or I may be wrong. How do you see it? After all, you are the one who must make the choice."

Civil Disobedience

My crucifixion was an act of civil disobedience. I accepted torture and death, because I refused to speak anything but the truth that I knew in my heart.

To stand for the truth in the face of opposition is not an easy thing to do. If one values one's body too much, one cannot do it. Only one who values the truth above all else can put himself in harm's way for the sake of what he believes in.

Surely, I am not the only one you know who has done that. There are many you know who have risen above their fear to stand up for what they believe in.

Non-Violence

Standing up for truth is a forceful act, but it is not a violent one. One who stands for truth must do so in a loving way or it is not truth s/he stands for.

There will be times when you must stand up for yourself and for others who are being mistreated. You cannot live your life in a state of fear, cowering in a corner while others make decisions for you. You must stand up and be counted.

But please do so lovingly, compassionately, respectfully. Do it knowing that there is no enemy out there. Each brother or sister, no matter how angry, fearful or distraught, deserves your support and your respect. And how you act means as much as what you do or what you say.

Inner Authority

I demonstrate to you the power that manifests when one listens to one's inner voice and follows it, even when other people judge or object. I stand for the inner authority of the universal heart-mind which holds everyone in equal reverence. I know that when you trust the divine within, you cannot help but become authentic.

I have tried to show you a way of cutting yourself loose from parental authority, cultural authority, and religious authority. I have told you that the laws and customs of men and women are limited by the conditions of their experience. They cannot see beyond them.

I have asked you to have the courage to stand alone so you can shed the narrow identifications that prevent you from knowing who you are. I have asked you to leave your homes and your work, so that you could stand back and look at your life from a distance, seeing the self-limiting, fear-based patterns of relating. I have asked you to stand back so that you would realize that you do not have to sell yourself short.

A man and a woman must leave the home of their parents and open to new experiences if they are to create a home of their own. For the same reason, you must leave your school, your career, your religion, and your relationship so that you can discover who you are apart from the conditions of your life.

You are not just a son or a daughter, a husband or a wife, a carpenter or a plumber, a black person or a white person, a Christian or a Jew. Yet if you identify with these roles, you will not discover the essence within you that goes beyond them. Nor will you find a way to transcend the inevitable division these external definitions will create in your life.

I have asked you to listen to others with respect, but never to accept their ideas and opinions as an authority in your life. I have asked you to find that authority within, even though no one else in your life agrees with it. And I have asked you to follow that inner authority even in the face of outright criticism from your friends, your family, your church, your race, your political party, and your country.

I have asked you to stand alone, not because I wish to isolate you, but so you can know the truth and anchor in it. For there will be times when you will have to stand in that truth in the midst of a crowd of people who would ignore it, scapegoating and condemning their brothers and sisters, as they once condemned me. There will be times, my friend, when you will be the voice in the wilderness that helps people find their way back home. And you could not become that voice if you did not leave home and learn to stand alone with the truth.

Truth, Essence and Love

Truth lies in the heart along with essence and love. They can be embodied and expressed only when you do not need to be right, loved back or approved of.

To reach truth, love, and essence, you must refuse to be satisfied with their imitations. If you accept conditional love, you will not experience love without conditions. If you accept any form of dogma, judgment or prejudice as truth, you will not know the pure truth of the heart. If you seek the approval of other men and women and are attached to the way they receive you, you will not express your essential self even when it is called for.

If you mistake the false for the true, you cannot affirm what is true or deny what is false. That, my friends, is the difficulty of words and concepts. To penetrate to the core, you must go beyond words and concepts.

When you speak of love, please ask yourself "Is my love free of conditions?" When you speak of truth, please ask yourself "Is my truth free of judgment or opinion?" When you speak of essence, ask "Am I attached to the way people perceive or receive me?"

Freedom to be yourself requires more detachment than you think. As long as you want something from anyone, you cannot be yourself. Only when you want nothing in particular from anyone are you free to be yourself and to interact honestly and authentically with others.

I do not say this to discourage you, but to prepare you for the depth and breadth of the journey you are on. To be a self-realized person requires that you disconnect from all expectations and conditions whether they come from you or from another.

Trusting the Source

Trust in your connection to the Source of all things. You have everything you need to be guided wisely in your life. You are no further away from God than I am. You don't need me to bring you to the feet of the Divine. You are already there.

God is incapable of moving away from you. When you do not feel the presence, it is because you have moved away. You have given your power to some earthly authority. You have left the place of the indwelling God in search of something special in the world. That search always comes up empty, but that doesn't mean that you won't keep trying to find the answer somewhere outside of yourself.

If you have a teacher who empowers you, I am happy. It does not matter to me if that teacher is a Buddhist or a Jew, a Christian or a Moslem, a shaman or a business-man. If you are learning to trust yourself, if you are becoming more open in your mind and your heart, then I am happy for you. It does not matter what specific path you are on, what symbols you believe in, or what scrolls you consider sacred. I look to the fruit of your beliefs to see if you are stepping into your divinity or giving your power away to someone else.

No, I do not want your exclusive allegiance. I simply ask you to choose a teacher who empowers you to dis-cover truth within your own heart, for there alone will you find it. When you give your power away, to me or to anyone else, I know that you have not heard me.

Your path has its own simple beauty and mystery. It is never what you think it is. Yet it is never beyond your ability to intuit the next step.

※

You prepare the inner temple for God to come. And who, my friends, is God but the One in you who knows and understands, the One who loves and accepts you without conditions, under all circumstances, now and for all time?

That being is not outside of you, but in your heart of hearts. When you ask sincerely, this is the One who answers. When you knock, this is the One who opens the door.

※

Deeply imbedded in your psyche is the call to awaken. It does not sound like the call that anyone else hears. If you are listening to others, you will not hear the call.

But once you hear it, you will recognize that others hear it too, in their own way. And you will be able to join with them in simple support. Blessing them, you bless yourself. Setting them free to travel their own path, you will set yourself free to travel yours.

Form and the Formless

The Body

Whenever I point out the inherent limitations of the physical body, someone inevitably interprets my statements to mean "the body is bad, inferior, or evil." This need to reject the body is a form of attachment to it. Where there is resistance to desire, desire itself is made stronger.

The body is not bad or inferior in any way. It is simply temporal. You will never find ultimate meaning by satisfying its needs. Nor might I add will you find ultimate meaning by denying its needs. Taking care of the body is an act of grace. Preoccupation with bodily pleasures or pains is anything but graceful.

Being in the body is both a privilege and a challenge. Many lessons are learned thanks to the opportunity the body provides.

Yet you must remember that everything the body can do for you will one day be undone. The pleasures of food, drink, sex, sleep, entertainment, what will these mean when the body is no longer? To worship the body is as unhelpful as it is to demean it.

The body is a means. It is a vehicle for gathering experience. It has a purpose. I used my body to complete my mission here, just as you must use yours. I experienced physical joy and physical suffering, just as you no doubt have. Each person who comes into the body experiences ecstasy and pain, love and death.

The body is a vehicle. It is a means for learning. Please do not disrespect or demean it. Please do not make it into a god that you worship. Don't make it more or less important than it is.

When you enjoy and care for your body, it can serve you better. But no body is perfect. All bodies eventually break down. Bodies are not meant to last forever. Those who speak of physical immortality have missed the point entirely.

Your challenge is not to stay in your physical body forever. It is to surrender to your experience that it may be lifted up and guided by grace. Then, you will be an instrument of salvation for yourself and others.

I once asked you to be in the world but not of it. I suggested that you be in the body, honor it, use it as a vehicle for spreading love and acceptance, without being attached to it. I also asked you not to build your house on sand, where every storm takes its devastating toll. Some things are temporary and temporal, and some are eternal. The body is not eternal. The best it can be is a temporary servant.

Sexuality

Some people oppose healthy sexuality because they have trouble accepting their own sexuality. These people —including many clergy—would poison the waters for others. Pay them no mind. They have their own difficult lessons in this life.

The only sexual expression that is reprehensible is sex without love. Some people are addicted to this kind of object-oriented sex. They try to find their satisfaction through the pleasure of orgasm. This never works, because after the peak of every orgasm is the trough of existential contact with the partner. If you love the person you are with, the trough will be a peaceful, comforting space. If you do not love the person, the trough will feel hollow and uncomfortable.

Sex without love is ultimately unsatisfactory and addictive. More will always be needed. More sex, more partners, more stimulation. But more is never enough. When you engage in sexual activity with someone you do not love, you dishonor yourself and the other person.

Do not engage in sexual behavior with someone you don't love. Even if you are in a loving partnership, do not engage in sexual behavior when your heart is not open to your partner. Sex without love, under any guise, fragments the energy of your union and exacerbates your emotional wounds.

Let your lovemaking be a joyful act, an act of surrender to the Christ in yourself and your partner. Physical love is no less beautiful than other forms of love, nor can it be separated from them. Those who view physical love as unholy will experience it that way, not because it is, but because they perceive it that way.

When you are married, the urge to sexual union is an important part of the sacrament. Marriage is meant to be a full-chakra embrace. Sexual passion is part of a greater attraction to be with the person. Whenever it splits off, sex becomes an attack.

Some married people engage in non-loving, non-surrendered and non-devotional sex. This behavior is often the beginning of a process of fragmentation that culminates in infidelity.

When love is mutual and the partners are surrendered to each other emotionally, sexuality is completely uplifting and sacred. But when communication in the relationship becomes careless and shoddy, when time is not taken for one-to-one intimacy, the relationship becomes a shell in which one hides. Energy and commitment disappear from the relationship. And sex becomes an act of physical betrayal.

Abortion

"Is it ever right," you ask, "to take the life of an unborn child?" I must tell you that it is never right to take a life, under any circumstances. Does that mean that it will not happen? No, that is for sure. And when it does happen, one needs to have compassion for all those involved.

You do not live in a perfect world. To expect others to be perfect is to attack them. That is not my teaching. Even perceiving others as wrong is a form of attack.

Do not attack your brother or sister. Nothing good can come of it.

The Ego

Your ego is the part of you that doesn't know that you are loved. It can't give love, because it doesn't know it has love to give.

When you love and accept your ego, it recognizes that it has love. The contracted aspects of consciousness relax. Resistance ceases to be. As soon as ego recognizes it has love, it ceases to be ego.

Ego must die as ego to be reborn as love.

Now you know why most people resist enlightenment. The idea of waking up is scary to anyone who is still asleep.

Your fear of death and your fear of waking up are the same fear. The unlimited, universal Self is not born until the limited, temporal self dies.

Dying

Dying is one of the best ways to learn to be present. If you want to wake up quickly, try dying. When you are dying, you are aware of things in a way you never were before. You notice every breath, every nuance, every flower, every word or gesture of love.

Dying is like a crash course in waking up. Now that doesn't mean that everyone who dies wakes up. It just means they've taken the course.

Disengaging from meaningless identity is an inevitable aspect of the path back home. The less you have to protect, the more blissful your experience becomes.

While I would not go so far as to say "dying is fun," I would say that dying is "not fun" only because you are still hanging onto some shred of self-definition.

Unless You Die and Be Reborn

I have told you that unless you die and be reborn you cannot enter the kingdom of heaven. No one comes here to earth without suffering the pain of loss. Every identity you assume will be taken from you when it is time. Every person you love will die. It is just a matter of time. And it is just a matter of time before you too leave your body and the world behind.

All sacred teachings exhort you not to be attached to the things of this world, because they are not permanent. Yet you get attached nonetheless. That is part of the process of your awakening: getting attached and letting go, embracing and releasing. In this way, love is deepened and wisdom is born.

You will experience many small deaths in the course of your life, many times when you must let go of the arms that once comforted you and walk alone into the uncertain future. Every time you do so your fears will rise up and you will have to walk through them.

Don't be impatient. No one is reborn instantaneously. It takes time. It is a process. The tide goes out and comes back in. People let go of one attachment only to form another one that challenges them more. Life is rhythmic, but progressive. As earth and water breathe together, the shape of the beach changes. Storms come and go.

In the end, a profound peace comes and pervades the heart and mind. Finally, the ground of being has been reached. Here the changing waters come and go, and the earth delights in them as a lover delights in the playful touch of his beloved.

A deep acceptance is felt and, with it, a quiet recognition that all things are perfect as they are. This is grace, the presence of God come to dwell in your heart and in your life.

Permanence cannot be found at the level of form. All form is in essence a distortion of the original formlessness of the universe. What is all-inclusive, all-accepting, all-loving cannot be limited to form. Love is without conditions; that it to say it is without form.

You cannot avoid the death of the ego, nor can you avoid the death of the body. But these are not necessarily the same. Do not make the mistake of believing that your ego dies when your body does, or that your body dies when your ego does.

Ascension

When you act in a loving way and speak loving words, the Spirit dwells in you and is awakened in others. Then you are the light of the world, and physical reality does not seem as dense as it was before. This is the correct meaning of the word ascension.

When love is present, the body and the world are lifted up. They are infused with light, possibility and celebration of goodness. The world you see when Spirit is present in your heart and your life is not the same world that you see when you are preoccupied with your ego needs. The world that you see when you are giving love is not the same world that you see when you are demanding it.

If you want to go beyond the body, learn to use it in a loving way. Think and speak well of yourself and others. Be positive, constructive, helpful. Don't look for problems. Don't dwell on what seems missing. Give love at every opportunity. Bring it to yourself when you are sad. Bring it to others when they are doubting or negative.

Be the presence of love in the world. That is what you are. Everything else is an illusion.

A Life of Service

As soon as you begin to see that your needs are the same as the needs of others, the veil begins to lift. You stop needing special treatment. You stop giving others special treatment. What you want for one, you want for all. You do not make one person more important than others.

The perception of equality is the beginning of the transcendence of the body and the physical world. All bodies are essentially the same. All bodily needs are essentially the same. All emotional needs are essentially the same. All beliefs in separation are essentially the same.

When you no longer need to hold yourself separate from others, you can serve others without being attached. You can give without needing to know how the gift is being received.

Service is an opportunity, not a job description. You cannot serve and have an identity or an agenda. You can't serve and be attached to the outcome.

When you help someone else, you help yourself. You help your mother and father. You help your third cousin. You help the drunk on the street corner. Your help goes to those who need it.

Help has nothing to do with you as helper or helpee, other than your simple willingness to give and receive in the moment. Help is for one and for all. You cannot offer it to one without offering it to all. Nor can you offer it to all unless you offer it to one.

Two Worlds in One

It seems that there are two worlds, but truly there is only one. Fear is but the lack of love. Scarcity is but the lack of abundance. Resentment is but the lack of gratitude.

Something cannot be lacking unless it was first present in abundance. Without presence, absence has no meaning.

This is like a game of hide and seek. Someone has to hide first. Who will it be? Will it be you or me? Perhaps it will be the Creator Himself.

In truth, it matters not. When it is your turn, you will hide, and your brother will find you, as I found him. Every one gets a turn to hide and everyone eventually is found.

The world of duality emanates from wholeness and to wholeness returns. What is joined separates and comes together again. This is the nature of the human/divine dance.

Living in the Present Moment

Love Happens Now

When love is present, you don't worry about the future. When love is lacking, then you want guarantees about tomorrow.

Love comes into being right now. The alpha and omega of existence are present in this moment. There will never be more love than is possible here and now.

Do you hear that? The greatest love that you can attain is attainable right now. It cannot be experienced in the past and future.

Heaven is Here

You forgive not to gain salvation in the future, but to experience salvation right here, right now. Your entire spirituality is lived in this moment only. It has nothing to do with anything you have ever thought or felt in the past. It is happening right now, with the circumstance that lies before you.

If you could be without time for a single instant, you would understand your salvation. In that timeless moment, nothing you have said or done means anything. In that moment, there is nothing to own: no past, no future, no identity. There is just the moment of pure being, the moment you inhabit all the time without knowing it. Imagine that: you are already in heaven and do not know it!

You are in heaven, but heaven is not acceptable to you. Heaven does not support your ego, your schemes and your dreams. Heaven does not support your power struggles, your lessons, or even your forgiveness process.

Heaven does not support your soap opera of crime and punishment, sin and salvation. In heaven, there is nothing that needs to be fixed.

In this moment also, there is nothing that needs to be fixed. Remember this, and you are in the kingdom.

You experience darkness and scarcity only when you find fault with the situation you are presented with in the moment. When you see the situation and feel gratitude for it, you experience only bliss.

Do not try to move out of darkness. Do not try to move into bliss. Just be where you are and be willing to love and accept what's there.

Happiness happens only in the present moment. If you become concerned about whether you will be happy tomorrow or even five minutes from now, you won't be able to be happy now. Your scheming and dreaming take you away from your present happiness.

Please take a deep breath and come back into your heart. All of the chaos and confusion in your mind can be transcended through your simple decision to be wholly present and attentive right now. That is the miraculous truth.

✺

You think that somewhere along the line something in you got broken, or that you are missing some parts. But you have no missing or broken parts. All of your wholeness is fully present right now.

Freedom from the Past

I have told you that you are free to live whatever life you choose to live. "Fat chance!" you say, pointing to the chains on your feet.

"Who made those chains?" I ask.

"God did!" you angrily exclaim.

"No. It is not true. God did not make the chains. If He made them, you would never escape from the prison of your own beliefs."

✺

Until you can bless the past, you won't be free to leave it. You cannot "leave your nets" and take the fish with you. In time, the fish will rot and leave a terrible stench. For miles around, people will anticipate your arrival.

"The Fisherman is coming," they will say. Your past walks in front of you. This is not the way to freedom.

Throw the fish away. Give them their freedom so that you can claim your own.

Walking the Tightrope

The more attached you are to the past, or the more invested you are in a future outcome, the harder it is for you to accept "what is" and work with it.

What happened in the past can prejudice you toward what is happening now. It can prevent you from opening fully to the present. For example, if you were hurt by someone in the past, you might be afraid to be in a relationship with someone else now.

Some things belong to the future, not to the present. For example, you might want to get married sometime in the future. But if you are always seeing your present relationship as a potential marriage, you may not give it a chance to unfold naturally.

The truth is that you don't know specifically what will happen in the future. You may have a general sense of the future, based on the way the present is unfolding. You may know what the next step is. But that's about all you can know right now.

To be in the present, you need to stay centered in what you know and put the past and the future aside. If you keep bringing the past in or trying to plan for the future, you will start getting behind or ahead of yourself. You will sow the seeds of conflict within and without.

So this is a balancing act. You need to walk the tightrope between the past and the future. And you can't expect to walk without tipping to one side or the other. But when you do, you must lean the other way, so that you can come back to center.

Centering means being present. It means staying with what you know and dropping what you don't know. You don't know that the past is going to repeat itself. You don't know that your present experience is going to extend into the future. Things may change or they may stay the same. Old patterns may dissolve or they may reappear. You don't know these things. All you know is how you feel about what's happening right now.

If you can stay with this, then you can be honest with yourself and with others about your experience. You can say what you are able to commit to and what you cannot commit to right now.

Things may change in the future, but you can't live right now hoping they are going to change. You must be where you are, not where you want to be.

This is difficult work. The past is saying "Don't open. It's too scary. Don't you remember what happened when…?" and the future is saying "This is taking so long, why don't you just jump in and do it?" The past is trying to hold you back and the future is trying to rush you, an interesting dilemma don't you think?

The truth is that you need to listen to both voices and reassure them that they have been heard. Then, you can rebalance and come back to center. Then, you can try to find a pace that feels good for right now.

That is what the tightrope walker must do. She can't worry about losing her balance in the past. She can't dream about a perfect performance in the future. She needs to focus on what's happening right now. She needs to put one foot in front of the other. Every step is an act of balance. Every step is a spiritual act.

Yesterday and Tomorrow

Many people go to psychics, astrologers, tarot card readers and so forth, hoping to find out what is going to happen in the future. However, the future cannot be predicted.

True, there are patterns that are set in motion in your life, but every moment offers you a new choice that can alter your destiny. Unfortunately, the more preoccupied you are in finding out what will happen to you in the future, the less attention you can give to the choices you need to make now.

An obsession with the past can be just as dysfunctional as a preoccupation with the future. Many people go to therapists or psychics looking for knowledge of the past which could explain problems in the present. They engage in a variety of forms of psychoanalysis, dream therapy, inner child work, hypnotherapy, past life regression and so forth. While this work may help some people move on in their lives, it becomes a quagmire for others. A tool meant to help becomes a dogma. A technique meant to assist you in discovering the source of your pain becomes an invitation to wallow in it and become its perpetual victim.

Very little is gained on the spiritual path as a result of these excursions into yesterday or tomorrow. The projected dramas of past or future are distractions that take you away from the real challenge of being present here and now.

Past Lives

Since "now" is the only time there is, all incarnations are simultaneous. All dreams of self are present in this dream. That is why it is not helpful to concern yourself with who you were in some past life. There are no past lives, any more than there are past experiences.

The belief in the past is what limits your ability to be fully present in the moment. And that presence is necessary if you are to wake up from the dream of self-abuse.

Do not go in search of memories from the past. If they come up, acknowledge them, be with them and integrate them. Do this not to empower the past, but to complete it, so that you can be present now. Anything that takes you away from your immediate communion with life is not helpful.

Once the past is released, it no longer exists in consciousness. Remember the question: if a tree falls in the forest and nobody hears it, did it make a sound? The answer is no. Without an experiencer, there is no experience.

That is why self-forgiveness works. When the experiencer ceases to relive the experience, the experience ceases to exist and the experiencer returns to the present innocent and unabused.

Are there past lives? Only if you remember them. And if you remember them, you will continue to live them until you come to forgiveness of yourself.

The key to all of this is simple: do not gather wood unless you want to make a fire. Do not stir the pot unless you want to smell the stew. Do not solicit the past unless you want to dance with it.

But if there is a fire in your house, you must pick up your things and leave. If the stew is boiling, you can't help but smell it. If the past is dancing in your mirror, you can't pretend to be in samadhi.

Resistance of experience creates endless detours. But so does seeking.

Do not resist. Do not seek. Just deal with what comes up as it arises.

Dropping Your Stories

You don't have to be concerned about what happened in the past or what will happen in the future. You don't need any more stories to put you to sleep.

Your stories of the past reinforce your fears and justify your rituals of self-protection. Whenever you connect with what you want, you also connect with all the reasons why you can't have it. You want to leave your job, but you can't.... You want to commit to this relationship, but you can't." On and on it goes.... the perpetual "Catch 22." You want to bring new energy into your life and hold onto your old habits at the same time. You want change, but you are afraid of it.

Your pain is a known quantity. You don't want to trade it for an unknown pain. You prefer a familiar suffering to an unfamiliar one. That's why your spiritual adult's heroic plan for the transformation of your life is inevitably undermined by the fears of your wounded child, who doesn't think s/he is lovable, and therefore cannot have a vision of a life without pain. To the wounded kid within, any promise of release from pain is a trick that entices you to let your defenses down and become vulnerable to attack.

Into this duplicitous environment of the psyche at war with itself then come a variety of professional fixers: psychiatrists, counselors, preachers, self-help gurus. Each claims to have the answer, but each solution offered and taken just compounds the problem.

Professional fixers believe your stories of brokenness and try to heal you. If your story isn't juicy enough, they help you make it more compelling. It's all about high drama, about sin and salvation. It never occurs to them or to you that maybe nothing is broken, that maybe there is nothing in you that needs to be fixed.

The external problems you perceive in your life are projections of the internal conflict: "I want but I cannot have." If you would allow yourself to have what you want, or if you would stop wanting it because you know you can't have it, this conflict would cease. Having what you want or accepting that you can't have it ends your conflict. It also ends your story.

There's no more drama of seeking once you have found love, joy, and happiness.... "And they lived happily ever after...." Story over. Drama complete. Now, what's next?

The truth is you are not ready to give up your dramas.

Your story has become part of your identity. Your pain is part of your personality. You do not know who you are without it. Letting your drama go means letting the past dissolve right here, right now.

If you can do that, it doesn't matter what happened in the past. It has no power. It doesn't exist any more. You are writing on a clean slate.

That means that right now you are totally responsible for what you choose. There are no more excuses. You can't blame what happens on the past or on your karma, because there is no more past, no more karma.

When you no longer interpret your life based on what happened yesterday or last year, what happens is neutral. It is what it is. There is no charge on it.

The freedom to be fully present and responsible right now is awesome. Very few people want it.

Most of you wear your past like a badge of honor. You stay in the drama because you love it. And so you have to heal all the make-believe wounds you think that you have. It doesn't matter that those wounds are not real. They are real enough to you.

And so the drama continues: "I seek but do not find. I want, but I can't have."

Freedom Vs Security

You want to be free, but you want your security too.

Try telling a person who is in prison getting three meals a day that freedom is its own security. S/he wants those three meals a day no matter what. Then s/he will talk about freedom.

When you are attached to what you already have, how can you bring in anything new in? To bring in something new, something fresh, something unpredictable, you must surrender something old, stale and habitual.

If you want the creative to manifest within you, you must surrender all that is not creative. Then in the space made by that surrender, creativity rushes in.

If the cup is full of old, cold tea, you cannot pour new, hot tea into it. First you have to empty the cup. Then you can fill it.

If you want to give up your drama, first find out what your investment is in it. What is your pay-off for not finding, not healing, not living happily ever after?

And then be honest. If you don't want to move through your pain, tell the truth. Say "I'm not ready to move through my pain yet." Don't say "I wish I could be done with my pain, but I can't be." That is a lie. You could be done with it, but you don't choose to be done. Perhaps you enjoy the attention you get being a victim.

You can't be on a spiritual path until you are done being a victim. When you learn to accept responsibility, there are no excuses. When you are not ready, you say "I am not ready." When you are ready, your actions flow from that readiness, and actions always speak louder than words.

Walking Through Closed Doors

Life has its own rhythm. If you are surrendered, you will find it. But surrendering is not so easy.

Surrendering means meeting each moment as new. And to do that, you cannot be attached to what just happened. You can appreciate it. You can savor it. But you must let it go where it will.

You can't control what happens. You can only be open to it or resist it. If you have expectations, you will be resisting. Don't resist. Don't have attachments to the past or expectations of the future.

Just be where you are. Bring everything into the now.

Bring the attachment, the expectations into the present. Be aware of your resistance. See the drama of your disappointment. See that you did not get what you wanted. See how it makes you feel. Watch it. Experience it. But don't lose yourself in the drama.

When you can see the drama without reacting to it, you can stay anchored in the here and now. You can remain present. You can see which doors are closed and which ones are open.

Please, don't try to walk through closed doors. You will hurt yourself unnecessarily. Even if you don't know why a door is closed, at least respect the fact that it is. And don't struggle with the doorknob. If the door was open, you would know it. Wanting it to be open does not make it open.

Much of the pain in your life happens when you attempt to walk through closed doors or try to put square pegs in round holes. You try to hold onto someone who is ready to go, or you try to get somebody to do something before s/he is ready. Instead of accepting what is and working with it, you interfere with it and try to manipulate it to meet your perceived needs.

Obviously, this doesn't work. When you interfere

with what is, you create strife for yourself and others. You trespass. You get in the way.

That is why awareness is necessary. When you know that things are not flowing, you need to step back and realize that your actions are not helpful. You need to stop, pause, and consider. You need to cease what you are doing because it is not working and you don't want to make the situation worse than it is.

After stopping, acknowledge your mistake, first to yourself and then to others. This is the forgiveness process in its most simple terms.

When you interfere in the natural order of things, there is suffering. As soon as you stop interfering, suffering stops.

The Fire of Change

Most external changes follow on internal shifts of allegiance and attention. When someone ceases to be committed to a relationship, a shift takes place. Energy is withdrawn from one direction and placed in a new direction.

You can argue until you are blue in the face about whether it is right or wrong that someone's commitment changes, but it won't do you any good. You cannot prevent other people from going forward in their growth, even if you don't agree with their decisions.

If you look deeply enough, you will see that every apparent "loss" you experience brings an unexpected gain. When one person leaves a relationship that is not growing into deeper intimacy, the other person is set free too.

In the same manner, when you cease to be committed to your career, it falls apart. It is no longer as challenging and fun as it used to be. You can blame this change on your boss, but you will be missing the whole point. The job no longer works because you are no longer giving it your love, your support, your commitment.

Holding onto the job or the relationship will not help you get on with your life. But don't be surprised if it takes a while to let go.

When something in your life is not working, you often try to fix it. Then, if that doesn't work, you may pretend for a while that it's fixed even though you know it isn't. Finally, you realize that your heart just isn't in the job or the relationship. That's when you are ready to let go of it.

Letting go is an act of substantial courage. There is always some degree of pain in the release of someone or something that once brought you joy and happiness. You will have to be patient and mourn the loss. But when your mourning is over, you will see things differently. Opportunities you never could have dreamed of will come into your life.

As the old dies, the new is born. The phoenix rises from the ashes of destruction.

The fire of change is never easy to weather. But if you surrender, the conflagration is quickly over. In the enriched soil, the seeds of tomorrow can be sown.

The Open Door

Your Angelic Nature

Angels are not seven-foot tall creatures with wings. They are beings who have learned to honor themselves. Because they have walked through the door, they can hold the door open for you.

Don't see angels outside of yourself. That is not where they will be found. They live in a dimension that you can touch only through your heart.

Waiting for the Open Door

When one door is closed, you must wait patiently for another door to open. As long as you forgive yourself and others, you won't have to wait too long. Only when you hold onto your grievances do the doors remain closed to you.

It isn't helpful to obsess about your mistakes and feel bad about them. Guilt doesn't help you act more responsibly toward others. But learning from your mistakes does help you take greater responsibility and move on with your life.

Adjustments of this kind are a natural part of living in

a harmonious way. You can't be right all of the time. You are going to make mistakes, but if you can acknowledge and correct these mistakes, then you can stay on track. The doors will keep opening to you.

Grace comes when correction is constant. Then, it does not matter how many times you stray from the path or put your feet in your mouth. You can laugh at your errors and put them behind you.

Guilt is not constructive. If there is nothing you can do to make the situation better, then just accept it as it is. Sometimes, there's nothing to be done. It's no one's fault. Life is just as it is. And that's okay.

In knowing that life is okay, no matter how ragged and unfinished it seems, there is room for movement. A shift can happen. A door can open.

The most important door is the one to your heart. If it is open, then the whole universe abides in you. If it is closed, then you stand alone against the world.

Trust, and the river flows through your heart. Distrust, and a dam holds the river back.

A heart in resistance gets tired quickly. Life wears heavily upon it. But a heart that is open is filled with energy. It dances and sings.

When the door in your heart is open, all the important doors open in the world. You go where you need to go. Nothing interferes with your purpose or your destiny. Everything that you are unfolds naturally in its own time, without struggle or restraint.

The Dance of Acceptance

Acceptance is a life-long dance. You get better at it the more you do it. But you never dance perfectly. Fear and resistance continue to come up and you do the best you can with them.

In the dance of acceptance, unconscious becomes conscious. Your fear becomes your partner.

You dance with the inside and outside. You dance with what happens and with what you think and feel about it. There is never a time when you can get off the dance floor and go and take a nap.

Sometimes you get tired and you proclaim "I shall dance no more." But then, unexpectedly, you fall in love, or someone makes you a business offer you can't refuse. As soon as you really understand that the *Emperor has no clothes*, his designer shows up with the latest fashions.

No matter how hard you try, you cannot get out of the drama. You can't stop the dance. It goes on with you or without you.

Mistakes are part of the dance. But some people don't know this. Their business fails or their partner leaves them and they blow their brains out. They play for very high stakes.

The unhappier you are, the harder the dance becomes, because you must dance with your unhappiness. That's why acceptance is so important as a spiritual practice. The more you accept your life as it is, the easier the dance becomes.

The Poetry of Being

The simple beauty and majesty of life is to be found in its cyclical rhythms: the rising and setting of the sun, the phases of the moon, the changes in the seasons, the beating of the heart, the rhythmic unfolding of the breath.

Repetition provides continuity, familiarity, and safety. Yet, many people now are disconnected from the rhythms of nature and their own bodies. This is one of the tragedies of contemporary life. The connection with the earth, the physical body, the breath, is disrupted.

Changes happen perpetually without the time to reflect on them and integrate them. Relationships begin and end before people can establish any kind of interpersonal flow. Emotional demands crater the landscape of the heart, tearing into the soft tissue. Trust is compromised, patience forgotten.

The more unstable life seems, the more people gravitate toward the "security" promised by authority figures. People marry authority figures. They elect them. They go to their churches and join their cults. Yet, gradually, all these authority figures are discredited and their followers must pick up the pieces of their lives.

All who seek the sky without getting roots in the earth will be beat up by their experiences. In time they will return, shovels in hand, and begin the work of planting.

All that is spinning out to heaven will fall to earth, abused, shattered, and forsaken. That which is rootless will learn to grow roots. That which has sought authority without will learn to find it within.

And then, with feet firmly planted in the earth, the eyes will notice the procession of sun and the moon. The senses will feel the rise of sap in the spring and the lifting of leaves in the fall. Blood and breath will be restored. Rhythm will return. Safety will be re-created where it authentically lies, in the heart of each person.

It is not just the reach of your hands toward the sky, but the rootedness of your feet in the ground that helps you bring heaven to earth. Spirituality is a living with, as well as a living for. It is the poetry of being, the rhythm of life unfolding in each person and each relationship, moment to moment.

When the Snow Falls

When the snow falls, it covers ground, plants, trees, houses and roads with a white mantle. Everything looks fresh, new, innocent. Forgiveness comes in the same way, undoing the grievances of the past, replacing judgments with acceptance. In the light of forgiveness, you see your problems and challenges differently. You feel capable of meeting your life just the way it is.

Walking out into the new snow, you leave fresh footprints behind you. No more hiding or pretending to hold back. You have ventured forth boldly and anyone can follow you.

Forgiveness is as far-reaching as the snow. It touches everything in your life. But you must be willing to receive it, as the ground receives the snowfall. You must be willing to be occupied and cleansed by something greater than you.

In every successful relationship, forgiveness is an ongoing practice. Without forgiveness, there can be no communion between people. Instead, old wounds will be aggravated by hidden resentments.

This will not do. Negative thoughts and feeling states must be cleared on no less than a daily basis. Do not go to sleep angry with each other. Do not let the sun rise or set without making peace. Nurture your relationships. Be ready to let go of thoughts and feelings that can only injure and separate.

In your dance together, find a way to soften and come together when you feel angry or hurt. Come to each other as equals and admit your fear. Surrender your need to be right and to make the other person wrong. You are both right in your desire to be loved and respected. You are both wrong in your attempt to blame the other person for your unhappiness.

Relationship is a dance in a theater of wounds. As hard

as you try to avoid hurting your brother, he continues to cry out in pain. Your fear is triggered by his fear and vice versa. It's no one's fault. That's just the way it is.

After you have danced enough, you no longer take the drama so personally. You just get better at dancing out of your pain toward your joy. When you do that, the whole atmosphere on stage changes. An option arises that was not seen before.

To some, the earthly journey seems to be an arduous trek through a veil of tears. But even to these travelers, there are moments when the sun comes out and rainbows arch across the sky, moments when the pain slips away and the heart is filled with unexpected joy. Even when the dance is difficult, one feels grateful for the opportunity to participate and to learn.

Life is essentially dignified. It is true that you resist and sometimes even refuse to learn your lessons. But learn them you do. You move onward and upward and, as you do, body and mind become imbued with Spirit. Once identified with a specific mindset and a specific body, you are eventually set free to love without conditions and to receive the love that is offered you without resisting or defending.

That is the nature of your journey here. It is a good journey. May you take the time to appreciate and enjoy it. May you open your eyes and see the sun peeking through the clouds. May you see the light reflected by the snow-covered ground and the white boughs of the pine trees: light sparkling in all directions, embracing all of you, right here, right now.

NEW TITLES FROM HEARTWAYS PRESS

Paul Ferrini's luminous new translation captures the essence of Lao Tzu and the fundamental aspects of Taoism in a way that no single book ever has!

THE GREAT WAY OF ALL BEINGS:
RENDERINGS OF LAO TZU
by Paul Ferrini
ISBN 1-879159-46-5
320 pages hardcover $23.00

The Great Way of All Beings: Renderings of Lao Tzu is composed of two different versions of Lao Tzu's masterful scripture *Tao Te Ching*. Part one, *River of Light*, is an intuitive, spontaneous rendering of the material that captures the spirit of the *Tao Te Ching*, but does not presume to be a close translation. Part Two is a more conservative translation of the *Tao Te Ching* that attempts as much as possible to stay with the words and images used in the original text. The words and images used in Part One leap out from the center to explore how the wisdom of the Tao touches us today. By contrast, the words and images of Part Two turn inward toward the center, offering a more feminine, receptive version of the material.

A Practical Guide to Realizing your True Nature

*"Enlightenment is the realization of the light that is within you.
It is the conscious recognition and acceptance of that light.
Enlightenment is discovering who you already are and being it fully."*

ENLIGHTENMENT FOR
EVERYONE
by Paul Ferrini
ISBN 1-879159-45-7
160 pages hardcover $16.00

Enlightenment is not contingent on finding the right teacher or having some kind
of peak spiritual experience. There's
nothing that you need to get, find or
acquire to be enlightened. You don't need
a priest or rabbi to intercede with God for you. You don't need a
special technique or meditation practice. You don't need to memorize scripture or engage in esoteric breathing practices. You simply
need to discover who you already are and be it fully. This essential
guide to self-realization contains eighteen spiritual practices that
will enable you to awaken to the truth of your being. This exquisite
hard-cover book will be a life-long companion and will make an
inspirational gift to friends and family.

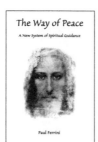

THE WAY OF PEACE
by Paul Ferrini

ISBN 1-879159-42-2
256 pages hardcover
$19.95

The Way of Peace is a simple method for connecting with the wisdom and truth that lie within our hearts. The two hundred and sixteen oracular messages in this book were culled from the bestselling *Reflections of the Christ Mind* series by Paul Ferrini.

Open this little book spontaneously to receive inspirational guidance, or ask a formal question and follow the simple divinatory procedure described in the introduction. You will be amazed at the depth and the accuracy of the response you receive.

Like the *I-Ching, the Book of Runes*, and other systems of guidance, *The Way of Peace* empowers you to connect with peace within and act in harmony with your true self and the unique circumstances of your life.

Special dice, blessed by the author, are available for using *The Way of Peace* as an oracle. To order these dice, send $3.00 plus shipping.

The Relationship Book You've Been Waiting For

THE SEVEN SPIRITUAL LAWS OF RELATIONSHIP: A GUIDE TO GROWTH AND HAPPINESS FOR COUPLES ON THE PATH

144 pages paperback $10.95
ISBN 1-879159-39-2

This simple but profound guide to growth and happiness for couples will help you and your partner:

- Make a realistic commitment to each other
- Develop a shared experience that nurtures your relationship
- Give each other the space to grow and express yourselves as individuals
- Communicate by listening without judgment and telling the truth in a non-blaming way
- Understand how you mirror each other
- Stop blaming your partner and take responsibility for your thoughts, feelings and actions
- Practice forgiveness together on an ongoing basis

These seven spiritual principles will help you weather the ups and downs of your relationship so that you and your partner can grow together and deepen the intimacy between you. The book also includes a special section on living alone and preparing to be in relationship and a section on separating with love when a relationship needs to change form or come to completion.

Our Surrender Invites Grace
GRACE UNFOLDING: THE ART OF
LIVING A SURRENDERED LIFE
96 pages paperback $9.95
ISBN 1-879159-37-6

As we surrender to the truth of our being, we learn to relinquish the need to control our lives, figure things out, or predict the future. We begin to let go of our judgments and interpretations and accept life the way it is. When we can be fully present with whatever life brings, we are guided to take the next step on our journey. That is the way that grace unfolds in our lives.

RETURN TO THE GARDEN REFLECTIONS OF THE CHRIST MIND, PART IV

$12.95, Paperback
ISBN 1-879159-35-X

"In the Garden, all our needs were provided for. We knew no struggle or hardship. We were God's beloved. But happiness was not enough for us. We wanted the freedom to live our own lives. To evolve, we had to learn to become love-givers, not just love-receivers.

We all know what happened then. We were cast out of the Garden and for the first time in our lives we felt shame, jealousy, anger, lack. We experienced highs and lows, joy and sorrow. Our lives became difficult. We had to work hard to survive. We had to make mistakes and learn from them.

Initially, we tried to blame others for our mistakes. But that did not make our lives any easier. It just deepened our pain and misery. We had to learn to face our fears, instead of projecting them onto each other.

Returning to the Garden, we are different than we were when we left hellbent on expressing our creativity at any cost. We return humble and sensitive to the needs of all. We return not just as created, but as co-creator, not just as son of man, but also as son of God."

*Learn the Spiritual Practice Associated
with the Christ Mind Teachings*

LIVING IN THE HEART THE
AFFINITY PROCESS AND THE PATH
OF UNCONDITIONAL LOVE AND
ACCEPTANCE

Paperback $10.95
ISBN 1-879159-36-8

The long awaited, definitive book on the Affinity Process is finally here. For years, the Affinity Process has been refined by participants so that it could be easily understood and experienced. Now, you can learn how to hold a safe, loving, non-judgmental space for yourself and others which will enable you to open your heart and move through your fears. The Affinity Process will help you learn to take responsibility for your fears and judgments so that you won't project them onto others. It will help you learn to listen deeply and without judgment to others. And it will teach you how to tell your truth clearly without blaming others for your experience.

Part One contains an in-depth description of the principles on which the Affinity Process is based. Part Two contains a detailed discussion of the Affinity Group Guidelines. And Part Three contains a manual for people who wish to facilitate an Affinity Group in their community.

If you are a serious student of the Christ Mind teachings, this book is essential for you. It will enable you to begin a spiritual practice which will transform your life and the lives of others. It will also offer you a way of extending the teachings of love and forgiveness throughout your community.

Now Finally our Bestselling Title on Audio Tape

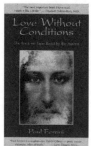

LOVE WITHOUT CONDITIONS,
REFLECTIONS OF THE CHRIST
MIND, PART I

by Paul Ferrini
The Book on Tape Read by the Author
2 Cassettes, Approximately 3.25 hours
ISBN 1-879159-24-4 $19.95

Now on audio tape: the incredible book from Jesus calling us to awaken to our own Christhood. Listen to this gentle, profound book while driving in your car or before going to sleep at night. Elisabeth Kubler-Ross calls this "the most important book I have read. I study it like a Bible." Find out for yourself how this amazing book has helped thousands of people understand the radical teachings of Jesus and begin to integrate these teachings into their lives.

With its heartfelt combination of sensuality and spirituality, Paul Ferrini's poetry has been compared to the poetry of Rumi.

CROSSING THE WATER: POEMS
ABOUT HEALING
AND FORGIVENESS IN OUR
RELATIONSHIPS

The time for healing and reconciliation has come, Ferrini writes. Our relationships help us heal childhood wounds, walk through our deepest fears, and cross over the water of our emotional pain. Just as the rocks in the river are pounded and caressed to rounded stone, the rough edges of our personalities are worn smooth in the context of a committed relationship. If we can keep our hearts open, we can heal together, experience genuine equality, and discover what it means to give and receive love without conditions.

With its heartfelt combination of sensuality and spirituality, Paul Ferrini's poetry has been compared to the poetry of Rumi. These luminous poems demonstrate why Paul Ferrini is first a poet, a lover and a mystic. Come to this feast of the beloved with an open heart and open ears. 96 pp. paper ISBN 1-879159-25-2 $9.95.

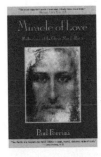

MIRACLE OF LOVE: REFLECTIONS OF THE CHRIST MIND, PART III

In this volume of the Christ Mind series, Jesus sets the record straight regarding a number of events in his life. He tells us: "I was born to a simple woman in a barn. She was no more a virgin than your mother was." Moreover, the virgin birth was not the only myth surrounding his life and teaching. So were the concepts of vicarious atonement and physical resurrection.

Relentlessly, the master tears down the rigid dogma and hierarchical teachings that obscure his simple message of love and forgiveness. He encourages us to take him down from the pedestal and the cross and see him as an equal brother who found the way out of suffering by opening his heart totally. We too can open our hearts and find peace and happiness. "The power of love will make miracles in your life as wonderful as any attributed to me," he tells us. "Your birth into this embodiment is no less holy than mine. The love that you extend to others is no less important than the love I extend to you." 192 pp. paper ISBN 1-879159-23-6 $12.95.

ILLUMINATIONS ON THE ROAD TO NOWHERE

There comes a time for all of us when the outer destinations no longer satisfy and we finally understand that the love and happiness we seek cannot be found outside of us. It must be found in our own hearts, on the other side of our pain. "The Road to Nowhere is the path through your heart. It is not a journey of escape. It is a journey through your pain to end the pain of separation."

This book makes it clear that we can no longer rely on outer teachers or teachings to find our spiritual identity. Nor can we find who we are in relationships where boundaries are blurred and one person makes decisions for another. If we want to be authentic, we can't allow anyone else to be an authority for us, nor can we allow ourselves to be an authority for another person.

Authentic relationships happen between equal partners who take responsibility for their own consciousness and experience. When their buttons are pushed, they are willing to look at the obstacles they have erected to the experience of love and acceptance. As they understand and surrender the false ideas and emotional reactions that create separation, genuine intimacy becomes possible, and the sacred dimension of the relationship is born. 160 pp. paper ISBN 1-879159-44-9 $12.95

THE ECSTATIC MOMENT: A PRACTICAL MANUAL FOR OPENING YOUR HEART AND STAYING IN IT.

A simple, power-packed guide that helps us take appropriate responsibility for our experience and establish healthy boundaries with others. Part II contains many helpful exercises and meditations that teach us to stay centered, clear and open in heart and mind. The Affinity Group Process and other group practices help us learn important listening and communication skills that can transform our troubled relationships. Once you have read this book, you will keep it in your briefcase or on your bedside table, referring to it often. You will not find a more practical, down to earth guide to contemporary spirituality. You will want to order copies for all your friends. 128 pp. paper   ISBN 1-879159-18-X $10.95

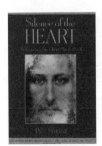

THE SILENCE OF THE HEART: REFLECTIONS OF THE CHRIST MIND, PART II

A powerful sequel to Love Without Conditions. John Bradshaw says: "with deep insight and sparkling clarity, this book demonstrates that the roots of all abuse are to be found in our own self-betrayal. Paul Ferrini leads us skillfully and courageously beyond shame, blame, and attachment to our wounds into the depths of self-forgiveness...a must read for all people who are ready to take responsibility for their own healing." 218 pp. paper. ISBN 1-879159-16-3 $14.95

LOVE WITHOUT CONDITIONS: REFLECTIONS OF THE CHRIST MIND, PART I

An incredible book from Jesus calling us to awaken to our Christhood. Rarely has any book conveyed the teachings of the master in such a simple but profound manner. This book will help you to bring your understanding from the head to the heart so that you can model the teachings of love and forgiveness in your daily life. 192 pp. paper ISBN 1-879159-15-5 $12.00

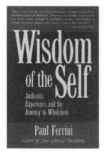

THE WISDOM OF THE SELF

This ground-breaking book explores our authentic experience and our journey to wholeness. "Your life is your spiritual path. Don't be quick to abandon it for promises of bigger and better experiences. You are getting exactly the experiences you need to grow. If your growth seems too slow or uneventful for you, it is because you have not fully embraced the situations and relationships at hand...To know the Self is to allow everything, to embrace the totality of who we are, all that we think and feel, all of our fear, all of our love." 229 pp. paper ISBN 1-879159-14-7 $12.00

THE TWELVE STEPS OF FORGIVENESS

A practical manual for healing ourselves and our relationships. This book gives us a step-by-step process for moving through our fears, projections, judgments, and guilt so that we can take responsibility for creating the life we want. With great gentleness, we learn to embrace our lessons and to find equality with others. A must read for all in recovery and others seeking spiritual wholeness. 128 pp. paper ISBN 1-879159 10 4 $10.00

THE WOUNDED CHILD'S JOURNEY: INTO LOVE'S EMBRACE

This book explores a healing process in which we confront our deep-seated guilt and fear, bringing love and forgiveness to the wounded child within. By surrendering our judgments of self and others, we overcome feelings of separation and dismantle co-dependent patterns that restrict our self-expression and ability to give and receive love. 225pp. paper ISBN 1-879159-06-6 $12.00

THE BRIDGE TO REALITY

A Heart-Centered Approach to A Course in Miracles and the Process of Inner Healing. Sharing his experiences of spiritual awakening, Paul emphasizes self-acceptance and forgiveness as cornerstones of spiritual practice. Presented with beautiful photos, this book conveys the essence of The Course as it is lived in daily life. 192 pp. paper ISBN 1-879159-03-1 $12.00

FROM EGO TO SELF

108 illustrated affirmations designed to offer you a new way of viewing conflict situations so that you can overcome negative thinking and bring more energy, faith and optimism into your life. 144 pp. paper ISBN 1-879159-01-5 $10.00

VIRTUES OF THE WAY

A lyrical work of contemporary scripture reminiscent of the Tao Te Ching. Beautifully illustrated, this inspirational book will help you cultivate the spiritual values required to fulfill your creative purpose and live in harmony with others. 64 pp. paper ISBN 1-879159-02-3 $7.50

THE BODY OF TRUTH

A crystal clear introduction to the universal teachings of love and forgiveness. This book traces all forms of suffering to negative attitudes and false beliefs, which we have the ability to transform. 64 pp. paper ISBN 1-879159-02-3 $7.50

AVAILABLE LIGHT

Inspirational, passionate poems dealing with the work of inner integration, love and relationships, death and re-birth, loss and abundance, life purpose and the reality of spiritual vision. 128 pp. paper ISBN 1-879159-05-8 $12.00

Poetry and Guided Meditation Tapes   by Paul Ferrini

THE POETRY OF THE SOUL

With its heartfelt combination of sensuality and spirituality, Paul Ferrini's poetry has been compared to the poetry of Rumi. These luminous poems read by the author demonstrate why Paul Ferrini is first a poet, a lover and a mystic. Come to this feast of the beloved with an open heart and open ears. With Suzi Kesler on piano. $10.00 ISBN 1-879159-26-0

THE CIRCLE OF HEALING

The meditation and healing tape that many of you have been seeking. This gentle meditation opens the heart to love's presence and extends that love to all the beings in your experience. A powerful tape with inspirational piano accompaniment by Michael Gray. ISBN 1-879159-08-2 $10.00

HEALING THE WOUNDED CHILD

A potent healing tape that accesses old feelings of pain, fragmentation, self-judgment and separation and brings them into the light of conscious awareness and acceptance. Side two includes a hauntingly beautiful "inner child" reading from The Bridge to Reality with piano accompaniment by Michael Gray. ISBN 1-879159-11-2 $10.00

FORGIVENESS: RETURNING TO THE ORIGINAL BLESSING

A self healing tape that helps us accept and learn from the mistakes we have made in the past. By letting go of our judgments and ending our ego-based search for perfection, we can bring our darkness to the light, dissolving anger, guilt, and shame. Piano accompaniment by Michael Gray. ISBN 1-879159-12-0 $10.00

Paul Ferrini Talks and Workshop Tapes

ANSWERING OUR OWN CALL FOR LOVE

A Sermon given at the Pacific Church of Religious Science in San Diego, CA November, 1997

Paul tells the story of his own spiritual awakening: his Atheist upbringing, how he began to open to the presence of God, and his connection with Jesus and the Christ Mind teaching. In a very clear, heart-felt way, Paul presents to us the spiritual path of love, acceptance, and forgiveness. 1 Cassette $10.00 ISBN 1-879159-33-3

THE ECSTATIC MOMENT

A workshop given by Paul in Los Angeles at the Agape International Center of Truth, May, 1997

Shows us how we can be with our pain compassionately and learn to nurture the light within ourselves, even when it appears that we are walking through darkness. Discusses subjects such as living in the present, acceptance, not fixing self or others, being with our discomfort and learning that we are lovable as we are. 1 Cassette $10.00 ISBN 1-879159-27-9

HONORING SELF AND OTHER

A Workshop at the Pacific Church of Religious Science in San Diego, November, 1997

Helps us understand the importance of not betraying ourselves in our relationships with others. Focuses on understanding healthy boundaries, setting limits, and saying no to others in a loving way. Real life examples include a woman who is married to a man who is chronically critical of her, and a gay man who wants to tell his judgmental parents that he has AIDS. 1 Cassette $10.00 ISBN 1-879159-34-1

SEEK FIRST THE KINGDOM

Two Sunday Messages given by Paul: the first in May, 1997 in Los Angeles at the Agape Int'l. Center of Truth, and the second in September, 1997 in Portland, OR at the Unity Church.

Discusses the words of Jesus in the Sermon on the Mount: "Seek first the kingdom and all else will be added to you." Helps us understand how we create the inner temple by learning to hold our judgments of self and other more compassionately. The love of God flows through our love and acceptance of ourselves. As we establish our connection to the divine within ourselves, we don't need to look outside of ourselves for love and acceptance. Includes fabulous music by The Agape Choir and Band. 1 Cassette $10.00 ISBN 1-879159-30-9

Double Cassette Tape Sets

ENDING THE BETRAYAL OF THE SELF

A Workshop given by Paul at the Learning Annex in Toronto, April, 1997

A roadmap for integrating the opposing voices in our psyche so that we can experience our own wholeness. Delineates what our responsibility is and isn't in our relationships with others, and helps us learn to set clear, firm, but loving boundaries. Our relationships can become areas of sharing and fulfillment, rather than mutual invitations to co-dependency and self betrayal. 2 Cassettes $16.95 ISBN 1-879159-28-7

RELATIONSHIPS: CHANGING PAST PATTERNS

A Talk with Questions and Answers Given at the Redondo Beach Church of Religious Science, November, 1997

Begins with a Christ Mind talk describing the link between learning to love and accept ourselves and learning to love and accept others. Helps us understand how we are invested in the past and continue to replay our old relationship stories. Helps us get clear on what we want and understand how to be faithful to it. By being totally committed to ourselves, we give birth to the beloved within and also without. Includes an in-depth discussion about meditation, awareness, hearing our inner voice, and the Affinity Group Process. 2 Cassettes $16.95 ISBN 1-879159-32-5

RELATIONSHIP AS A SPIRITUAL PATH

A workshop given by Paul in Los Angeles at the Agape Int'l. Center of Truth, May, 1997

Explores concrete ways in which we can develop a relationship with ourselves and learn to take responsibility for our own experience, instead of blaming others for our perceived unworthiness. Also discussed: accepting our differences, the new paradigm of relationship, the myth of the perfect partner, telling our truth, compassion vs. rescuing, the unavailable partner, abandonment issues, negotiating needs, when to say no, when to stay and work on a relationship and when to leave. 2 Cassettes $16.95 ISBN 1-879159-29-5

OPENING TO CHRIST CONSCIOUSNESS

A Talk with Questions & Answers at Unity Church, Tustin, CA November, 1997

Begins with a Christ Mind talk giving us a clear picture of how the divine spark dwells within each of us and how we can open up to God-consciousness on a regular basis. Deals with letting go and forgiveness in our relationships with our parents, our children and our partners. A joyful, funny, and scintillating tape you will want to listen to many times. 2 Cassettes $16.95 ISBN 1-879159-31-7

RISEN CHRIST POSTERS AND NOTECARDS

11"x17" Poster

suitable for framing

ISBN 1-879159-19-8 $10.00

Set of 8
Notecards with
Envelopes
ISBN 1-879159-
20-1 $10.00

ECSTATIC MOMENT POSTERS AND NOTECARDS

8.5"x11" Poster
suitable for framing
ISBN 1-879159-21-X $5.00

Set of 8 Notecards
with Envelopes
ISBN 1-879159-22-8
$10.00

HEARTWAYS PRESS ORDER FORM

Name_____

Address _____

City _____State _____Zip _____

Phone/Fax_____Email _____

BOOKS BY PAUL FERRINI

The Great Way of All Beings:

   Renderings of Lao Tzu Hardcover ($23.00)   __

Enlightenment for Everyone Hardcover ($16.00)   __

Taking Back Our Schools ($10.95)   __

The Way of Peace Hardcover ($19.95)   __

   Way of Peace Dice ($3.00)   __

Illuminations on the Road to Nowhere ($12.95)   __

Reflections of the Christ Mind: The Present Day

   Teachings of Jesus Hardcover ($19.95)   __

Creating a Spiritual Relationship ($10.95)   __

Grace Unfolding:: A Surrendered Life ($9.95)   __

Return to the Garden ($12.95)   __

Living in the Heart ($10.95)   __

Miracle of Love ($12.95)   __

Crossing the Water ($9.95)   __

The Ecstatic Moment ($10.95)   __

The Silence of the Heart ($14.95)   __

Love Without Conditions ($12.00)   __

The Wisdom of the Self ($12.00)   __

The Twelve Steps of Forgiveness ($10.00)   __

The Circle of Atonement ($12.00)   __

The Bridge to Reality ($12.00)   __

From Ego to Self ($10.00)   __

Virtues of the Way ($7.50)   __

The Body of Truth ($7.50)   __

Available Light ($10.00)   ___

AUDIO TAPES BY PAUL FERRINI

The Circle of Healing ($10.00) _____

Healing the Wounded Child ($10.00) _____

Forgiveness: The Original Blessing ($10.00) _____

The Poetry of the Soul ($10.00) _____

Seek First the Kingdom ($10.00) _____

Answering Our Own Call for Love ($10.00) _____

The Ecstatic Moment ($10.00) _____

Honoring Self and Other ($10.00) _____

Love Without Conditions ($19.95) 2 tapes _____

Ending the Betrayal of the Self ($16.95) 2 tapes _____

Relationships: Changing Past Patterns ($16.95) 2 tapes _____

Relationship As a Spiritual Path ($16.95) 2 tapes _____

Opening to Christ Consciousness ($16.95) 2 tapes _____

POSTERS AND NOTECARDS

Risen Christ Poster 11"x17" ($10.00) _____

Ecstatic Moment Poster 8.5"x11" ($5.00) _____

Risen Christ Notecards 8/pkg ($10.00) _____

Ecstatic Moment Notecards 8/pkg ($10.00) _____

SHIPPING

($2.50 for first item, $1.00 each additional item. _____

Add additional $1.00 for first class postage _____

and an extra $1.00 for hardcover books.) _____

MA residents please add 5% sales tax. _____

Please allow 1-2 weeks for delivery   TOTAL _____

Send Order To: Heartways Press P. O. Box 99,
Greenfield, MA 01302-0099   413-774-9474
Toll free: 1-888-HARTWAY (Orders only)